RICHARD WRIGHT

In the same series:

SAUL BELLOW   *Brigitte Scheer-Schäzler*
BERTOLT BRECHT   *Willy Haas*
ALBERT CAMUS   *Carol Petersen*
WILLA CATHER   *Dorothy Tuck McFarland*
FRIEDRICH DÜRRENMATT   *Armin Arnold*
T. S. ELIOT   *Joachim Seyppel*
WILLIAM FAULKNER   *Joachim Seyppel*
MAX FRISCH   *Carol Petersen*
MAKSIM GORKI   *Gerhard Habermann*
GÜNTER GRASS   *Kurt Lothar Tank*
PETER HANDKE   *Nicholas Hern*
ERNEST HEMINGWAY   *Samuel Shaw*
HERMANN HESSE   *Franz Baumer*
JAMES JOYCE   *Armin Arnold*
FRANZ KAFKA   *Franz Baumer*
SINCLAIR LEWIS   *James Lundquist*
GEORG LUKÁCS   *Ehrhard Bahr and
Ruth Goldschmidt Kunzer*
THOMAS MANN   *Arnold Bauer*
EUGENE O'NEILL   *Horst Frenz*
JOSÉ ORTEGA Y GASSET   *Franz Niedermayer*
EZRA POUND   *Jeannette Lander*
RAINER MARIA RILKE   *Arnold Bauer*
JEAN-PAUL SARTRE   *Liselotte Richter*
ISAAC BASHEVIS SINGER   *Irving Malin*
THORNTON WILDER   *Hermann Stresau*
THOMAS WOLFE   *Fritz Heinrich Ryssel*

Modern Literature Monographs

RICHARD WRIGHT

David Bakish

Frederick Ungar Publishing Co.
New York

Second Printing, 1974

Copyright © 1973 by David Bakish
Printed in the United States of America
Library of Congress Catalog Card Number: 71-190353
ISBN: 0-8044-2015-7 (cloth)

*For all
my students
in Bedford-Stuyvesant*

Acknowledgments

I would like to thank my editor, Stan Hochman, and the many people whose kind assistance I value: Hélène Bokanowski, Horace R. Cayton, Rev. O. B. Cobbins, Léon Damas, Michel Fabre, Minnie Eileen Farish, Gisele Freund, Herb Gentry, Walter Goldwater, Ollie Harrington, Leroy Haynes, Chester Himes, Edward Margolies, Gunnar Myrdal, Agnes Theo Pace, Mary Jane Pace, Margrit de Sablonière, Dr. Vladimir Schwarzmann, Lillian Perkins Scott, Mrs. Eddie McDill Shirley, William Gardner Smith, James Thomas, Margaret Walker, Rev. Clayton Williams, John A. Williams, Ellen Wright, and the Schomburg Collection of the New York Public Library.

A special word of thanks must go to Constance Webb for her help and encouragement.

Contents

	Chronology	ix
1	Mississippi and Chicago (1908-1937)	1
2	New York (1937-1947)	17
3	Paris (1947-1952)	55
4	Paris (1953-1957)	63
5	End of a Long Dream (1958-1960)	89
	Notes	101
	Bibliography	107
	Index	111

Chronology

1908: September 4, Richard Wright born near Natchez, Mississippi, son of an illiterate sharecropper, Nathaniel Wright, and a schoolteacher, Ella Wilson Wright.

1910: Younger brother, Alan, born.

1914: Family moves to Memphis, Tennessee, in search of work. Father abandons family.

1916: Richard enters Howard Institute, a grammar school. Mother ill, Richard and Alan placed by her in orphanage, remaining there six weeks, then all three move to Elaine, Arkansas, to live with Ella's sister, Maggie.

1918: Brief stay in West Helena, Arkansas, then the three-member family moves to Jackson, Mississippi, to live with Ella's mother. Richard's grandmother is a strict Seventh Day Adventist and begins to impose her harsh religious code upon everyone. Ella and her two sons return to West Helena that same year. Ella then suffers a paralytic stroke. Richard is sent to an uncle, one of Ella's brothers, Clark, in Greenwood, Mississippi, and Alan to Aunt

Maggie, now in Detroit. Ella, on a stretcher, is sent by train back to her mother in Jackson. Richard rejoins mother after a few months, where he watches her suffer a second stroke.

1920:   Richard is enrolled in a Seventh Day Adventist School in Huntsville, near Jackson. He's placed in a class taught by his Aunt Addie, severe in her religious devotion.

1921:   Richard attends the Jim Hill Public School, in Jackson, and is assigned to the fifth grade. He's shortly promoted to the sixth grade although his past schooling was almost nonexistent.

1923:   He enrolls at the Smith-Robertson Public School.

1924:   Local Negro newspaper, the *Southern Register,* prints his adventure story "The Voodoo of Hell's Half-Acre."

1925:   He graduates from the ninth grade at Smith-Robertson, first in his class. In the fall he registers for the tenth grade at Jackson's Lanier High School, but he quickly drops out, convinced the educational system had taught him nothing. After a few brief menial jobs in Jackson he moves to Memphis before the end of the year.

1927:   In December he arrives in Chicago, having saved money from odd jobs in Memphis. In Memphis he had begun reading literature, and was especially impressed by H. L. Mencken's essays and by the novels of Theodore Dreiser and Sinclair Lewis.

1928:   Doing more odd jobs, Wright studies for, and passes, a civil service examination and gets work as a post office clerk. What he earns is barely enough to support his mother and brother.

1929-1930: Immediately upon the crash of the stock market in November, and the beginning of the Depression, Wright loses his postal job and his mother becomes ill again. He gets a job with a Negro burial society and is dismayed to discover it is dishonest, a racket.

1931: He loses the job with the burial society and goes on relief. The relief office gets him several temporary jobs including work with the Federal Negro Theatre and later the Illinois Writers' Project, both WPA projects. *Abbott's Monthly* magazine publishes his short story "Superstition."

1932: After attending meetings of the John Reed Club, a literary group sponsored by the Communist Party, Wright joins the Communist Party.

1934-1937: Wright becomes a prolific writer of poems, short stories, and essays, many of these pieces published in leftist periodicals. In May 1937, he moves to New York, leaving behind in Chicago his mother and brother. He becomes the Harlem editor for the Communist newspaper, the *Daily Worker,* and helps edit the short-lived literary quarterly, *New Challenge.*

1938: Four of Wright's short stories are collected and published as *Uncle Tom's Children: Four Novellas.* This book wins a literary prize from *Story Magazine.*

1939: He writes an essay "Negroes in Manhattan" for a Federal Writers' Project, *New York City Guide.* Awarded a Guggenheim Fellowship, he is able to give more of his time to completing *Native Son*. He marries Rose Dhima Meadman, a white classical dancer, with Ralph Ellison best man.

1940:   March, publication of *Native Son*. The Book-of-the-Month Club chooses the novel as its March selection, ensuring large sales and publicity. An enlarged, second edition of his short story collection is published, *Uncle Tom's Children: Five Long Stories*. Wright has a measure of financial independence for the first time, and his name is now widely known. Trip to Mexico; dissatisfied with both Mexico and wife he returns alone to New York.

1941:   After divorcing Dhima, Wright marries Ellen Poplar, a white Communist Party organizer from Brooklyn. Benjamin Davis, Jr., important Party official, is a witness. Publication of *12 Million Black Voices: A Folk History of the Negro in the United States,* outgrowth of a WPA project. *Native Son* is produced on Broadway, the play written by Paul Green and Richard Wright, staged by Orson Welles's Mercury Theatre. On the strength of his novel the NAACP awards Wright its Spingarn Medal for noteworthy achievement by a Negro.

1942:   Julia, Wright's first of two children, is born.

1944:   Wright breaks with the Communist Party and publishes a two-part article in the *Atlantic Monthly,* "I Tried To Be a Communist." Publication of the novelette *The Man Who Lived Underground* in an anthology edited by Edwin Seaver, *Cross-Section 1944.*

1945: Publication of *Black Boy: A Record of Childhood and Youth.* It too receives wide publicity and sales from the Book-of-the-Month Club. Wright does the introduction for an important sociological study of Negro life in Chicago, *Black Metropolis,* by St. Clair Drake and Horace R. Cayton.

1946: May, trip with wife and daughter to Paris.

1947: January, return from Paris. August, second trip to Paris, with intention to make it home for himself, his wife and child.

1947-1952: No new books published. Comparatively little writing, preoccupation with Parisian cultural activities, friendship with French and African intellectuals. Second daughter, Rachel, born 1949. Working on film of *Native Son* in 1949-1950, as writer and actor, traveling to Argentina to shoot it after failing to interest Hollywood. Film released in 1951, an unpublicized, largely unseen failure.

1953: Publication of *The Outsider.* Trip to Africa.

1954: Publication of *Savage Holiday* and *Black Power: A Record of Reactions in a Land of Pathos.* Trip to Spain.

1955: Return to Spain, and travel to Indonesia for the Bandung Conference. French edition of report on the conference published in Paris before the American edition.

1956: *The Color Curtain: A Report on the Bandung Conference* published. Lecture tour to several Western European countries.

1957: Publication of *White Man, Listen!,* collection of lectures, and *Pagan Spain.*

1958: Publication of *The Long Dream.*

1959-1960:   Illness; trip to England; writing of poetry
after a lapse of many years; writing of an unpublished novel, *Island of Hallucination*;
preparation of a collection of short stories
for publication, *Eight Men* (1961); news of
the death of his mother in Chicago; death of
one of his closest friends, George Padmore,
in London. His own death, November 28,
1960, in Paris, at age 52.

1

*Mississippi
and Chicago
(1908-1937)*

There is more freedom in one square block of Paris than in the whole United States, Richard Wright would say to many of his friends, like himself black Americans who chose to live in Paris after World War II. Rue Monsieur le Prince lies in the heart of the left bank, in a quarter of the city traditionally favored by artists in rebellion against restraints upon man's freedom. Settled here, Wright could step outside himself and reassess what he had done.

Fighting free of a ghetto formed by poverty, ignorance, racial oppression, hatred, and fear, one black boy had entered the homes of hundreds of thousands of middle-class white Americans with the pleas and verbal assaults contained in an uncompromisingly brutal novel and an eloquently poetical autobiography that underscored the truth of that novel. For the first time since the Abolition struggle of one hundred years before, a Negro had captured the conscience of a nation.

Americans have always been proud of the country's rags-to-riches stories of personal success. Immigrants knew and believed in the American dream. Negroes also knew the stories, but were bitterly aware that their race was not to be included. Only a handful had filtered through the grate of success to create a black bourgeoisie, a middle class (anyone with two dollars in his pocket instead of one, generally a successful preacher or undertaker).

Richard Wright was incapable of becoming middle class because he could not rid himself of the anger within himself. He was a murderer: he had to kill the system that destroyed black minds and bodies. He could not rest content with money and fame, with merely titillating the slack consciences and mild curiosity of white readers. He had to rub their noses on the backside of the American dream, to show them that for some the dream was a nightmare. In almost all of Wright's fiction, a black man either kills or is killed, and the reader's head is pushed up close, so that he does not miss the detailed horror of the castration, the severed head, the lynching. In *Native Son* Bigger Thomas is characterized as having killed not once or twice, but—in his mind—many times. Wright too had "killed" many times, though to talk to the man, gentle and good-natured, most casual acquaintances would never have guessed.

Those who in the 1930's had read with horrified fascination the violent tales of *Uncle Tom's Children,* the many more who in the 1940's had been enthralled by *Native Son* and *Black Boy,* eventually turned away sated or revolted—or perhaps increasingly indifferent. Critics admired and admonished the almost fiendish intensity of the man, but sooner or later most shook their heads over a promising writer who had gone stale in Europe.

Any black man remaining in the United States after the age of thirty-five, Wright told friends, was bound to kill, be killed, or go insane. By settling in Paris in 1947, he was seeking to avoid these morbid alternatives while writing about the sociological and psychological roots of threatening mental illness. However, he could not completely shake off the sense of enslavement.

Born near Natchez, Mississippi, September 4, 1908, Richard Wright was educated largely through his own efforts, devouring book after book from public libraries that often did not welcome Negroes. The Communist Party philosophy caught his imagination and he joined the Party in Chicago (1932), writing articles and poems for the many left-wing and Communist Party periodicals that sprang up during the Depression of the 1930's. During this period he also found work with

riters' projects sponsored by the federal gov-
as it sought to give jobs to the critical numbers
icans out of work and starving.

ecause it did not allow him the freedom he de-
m___ ed as a writer, Wright left the Communist Party
in a widely-publicized break in 1944, but he remained
convinced that some adaptation of Marxist economic
philosophy could produce a better system than Capitalism. Later in a most prophetic way he would combine
Marxism with Black Nationalism, believing that the
nonwhite peoples of the world must unite economically
against the European-American exploiters who held
the power and arrogantly proclaimed their civilization
as superior. In *Black Power* (1954), *The Color Curtain* (1956), and *White Man, Listen!* (1957), he
would show an awareness that the race struggle was
only one part of the world struggle of oppressed peoples.

As Wright's nonfiction of the 1950's continued to
probe Marxist solutions to the world's economic problems, most of his fiction continued with the same basic
themes. Almost all the characters he described struggle, as he himself struggled, with ambiguous, unclear
identities, in an ambiguously gray, shadowy world. The
struggle is existential in a most natural, instinctive
sense; it is a search for self-definition. Blacks move
through a hostile environment in a dream-like trance,
not knowing the place of blackness in a culture that
equates whiteness with beauty, virtue, and purity. Images of light and dark, fire, death, religion, and flight
fill a semiconscious, intangible world between dreams
and reality.

Richard Wright did his best writing when in-
tensely angry, though the energy generated by this
anger often seemed dissipated in too many directions:

he was a political pamphleteer, journalist, lecturer, poet, novelist, sociologist, psychologist, historian, playwright, film writer, and actor. All his work, from the books to the speeches, contributes to the portrait of a man searching for a road, for a plan of action. Stages of the quest were *Uncle Tom's Children* (1938) and *Black Boy* (1945), with their Mississippi tar shacks and Jim Crow; *Native Son* (1940) and its reflection of the crude violence of Chicago's South Side; *The Outsider* (1953), a novel of intellectualized violence and New York sophistication; the travel books: *Pagan Spain* (1957), about a primitive Spain desiccated beyond bleeding; *Black Power* (1954), a vision of a muscle-flexing Africa; and *The Color Curtain: A Report on the Bandung Conference* (1956), an account of this historic meeting by anticolonial Asian and African nations. It is present in both the political articles of the 1930's and the later speeches and articles of the 1950's collected in *White Man, Listen!* (1957).

Sitting in a Paris café, Wright could look back, with anger and sorrow, at his youth. He could see his early struggle against poverty, fear, and racism. He could relive his efforts to educate himself and to express himself in writing. The son of an illiterate sharecropper father, who abandoned the family, and a sickly school-teacher mother, Richard had tasted the school system of Jackson, Mississippi. He had found that it offered no comfort to a black boy seeking to rise above the level of porter, servant, or shoeshine boy. A good student despite his lack of interest, he had graduated from the ninth grade first in a class of thirty black students. Then he quit school.

[T]he bleakness of the future affected my will to study. . . . [W]hat had I learned so far that would help me to make a living? Nothing. I could be a porter like my father before me, but what else? And the problem of living as a Negro was cold and hard. What was it that made the hate of whites for blacks so steady, seemingly so woven into the texture of things? What kind of life was possible under that hate? How had this hate come to be? Nothing about the problems of Negroes was ever taught in the classrooms at school; and whenever I would raise these questions with the boys, they would either remain silent or turn the subject into a joke. They were vocal about the petty individual wrongs they suffered, but they possessed no desire for a knowledge of the picture as a whole. Then why was I worried about it?

. . . Ought one to surrender to authority even if one believed that that authority was wrong? If the answer was yes, then I knew that I would always be wrong, because I could never do it. Then how could one live in a world in which one's mind and perceptions meant nothing and authority and tradition meant everything? There were no answers.[1]

After leaving school Wright held many jobs, all menial, far beneath his interests and ability. His failure to secure a skilled job, or even training for a skilled job, seemed to confirm his belief that public school programs were irrelevant to a black boy's future, that while Jewish, Italian, and Irish immigrants could use education and school degrees to advance their positions in American society, the same approach by a black man would only result in a more brutal rejection of his ambitions.

Wright describes in "The Ethics of Living Jim Crow"[2] how black men were denied jobs reserved for whites. In 1925, for example, he went to work for the American Optical Company in Jackson. The man who hired Wright was willing to teach him the trade and Richard was eager to learn, but the skilled white workers felt threatened, became vicious, and forced the black youth out of his job. Later that same year Wright moved to Memphis with the idea of working his way north to Chicago. He found that Memphis was not much different from Jackson.

Wright tells us in *Black Boy* how he circumvented Jim Crow in Memphis. Since the city's library refused books to Negroes unless they were fetching them for a white man, he forged notes and hungrily read H. L. Mencken, Sinclair Lewis, and Theodore Dreiser. The allusions Mencken made to countless other authors bewildered and fascinated Wright, and increased his already great desire to read.

In December 1927, at the age of nineteen, Wright moved further north, to Chicago. Would this great northern city mean greater freedom? Only on the surface. He would not live in fear of being lynched here, but he would soon find out that Jim Crow can take many forms. White people in positions of power still looked upon his intellectual curiosity and ambitions as unnatural impudence. Once more he had to accept jobs far beneath his ability and interests—washing dishes in a café, sorting letters in the post office—to support his mother and younger brother, Alan, who had joined him in Chicago.

For most people the Depression following the 1929 stock market crash was an overwhelming personal and national calamity. But for Richard Wright the Depression was a great stroke of good luck: with it came the rise of the Communist Party, which seemed to offer hope to the economically oppressed and a philosophy of reason to the intellectuals of the land. Down with the Capitalistic system! Down with bourgeois exploitation of the proletariat! Down with General Motors and up with the CIO and the AF of L! Wright joined the Communist Party.

With the Depression also came the first massive federal assistance program for the arts. The country's new president, Franklin D. Roosevelt, and the Democratic congress created Federal Writers' Projects. One of the many efforts to create jobs for the millions of unemployed, under the WPA (Works Progress Administration), the Writers' Projects gave a job to an unknown black man in Chicago. Richard Wright was named publicity agent for the Federal Negro Theatre and then given his first professional writing assignment.

The first work published by Wright had been a crude story he had written while sitting bored and daydreaming in an eighth-grade class. "The Voodoo of Hell's Half-Acre" was run in three installments by the local Negro newspaper, the *Southern Register* (Jackson, Miss.), in 1924. A second story, "Superstition," was published by *Abbott's Monthly,* a national magazine, in April 1931. Between 1931 and 1936, when a third short story was published, "Big Boy Leaves Home," Wright was making incredibly swift progress in developing his skill as a writer. "Superstition" was amateurish, "Big Boy Leaves Home" thoroughly professional.

Long before he became known for his stories, however, Wright achieved a small measure of fame among writers and left-wing intellectuals for his poetry. The fourteen poems published between 1934 and 1936 all appeared in periodicals closely alligned with the Communist Party: *Left Front, New Masses, The Anvil, Partisan Review,* and *International Literature.*

Lenin, revolution, and Chicago. In "I Tried To Be a Communist"[3] Wright tells of being invited by white postal clerks with whom he worked to discuss politics and the Communist Party. Later, at a meeting of the John Reed Club, a literary appendage of the Party, he was told he could be helped in his writing and taught to edit magazines as well. Someone gave him copies of *International Literature* and various political pamphlets. What he read excited and impressed him.

> The revolutionary words leaped from the page and struck me with tremendous force. . . . [M]y attention was caught by the similarity of the experiences of workers in other lands, by the possibility of uniting scattered but kindred peoples into a whole. It seemed to me that here at last, in the realm of revolutionary expression, Negro experience could find a home, a functioning value and role.[4]

In the nineteenth century Karl Marx had pointed out that the basic social problem the world must solve was the unfair economic advantage that permitted capital to exploit labor. Lenin and other Russian followers of Marx had put his theory of economics to the test in 1917 following the Bolshevik revolution. Now the American branch of the Communist Party was telling a black man that his road to freedom was the same road poor white men must be taught to travel.

Inspired by the Marxist literature he read, Wright composed "I Have Seen Black Hands," a poem of celebration and prophecy. "Feeling for the first time that I could speak to listening ears, I wrote a wild, crude poem in free verse, coining images of black hands playing, working, holding bayonets, stiffening finally in death. I felt that in a clumsy way it linked white life with black, merged two streams of common experience."[5]

> I am black and I have seen black hands
> Raised in fists of revolt, side by side
>   with the white fists of white workers,
> And some day—and it is only this which
>   sustains me—
> Some day there shall be millions and
>   millions of them,

On some red day in a burst of fists on
        a new horizon![6]

And in "Red Leaves of Red Books," published
less than a year after "I Have Seen Black Hands,"
Wright makes white-black cooperation in a Marxist
class struggle the central theme.

Turn
Red leaves of red books
Turn
In white palms and black palms
Turn
Slowly in the mute hours of the night
Turn
In the fingers of women and the fingers
        of men
In the fingers of the old and the
        fingers of the young[7]

New Masses, an official Communist Party journal
of opinion, published these two poems and several others; *Left Front,* a periodical published by the John
Reed Club of Chicago, and which Wright helped to
edit, printed two of his poems; and still other Marxist
periodicals encouraged him to write. *Partisan Review*—
which began publication as "A Bi-Monthly of Revolu-
tionary Literature," produced by the John Reed Club
of New York—first published what has become Wright's
most widely anthologized poem: "Between the World
and Me."[8] It describes in a painfully concrete and detailed first-person account the lynching of a Negro, the
torturing and burning of his flesh.

There was a charred stump of a sapling pointing
        a blunt finger accusingly at the sky.
There were torn tree limbs, tiny veins of burnt
        leaves, and a scorched coil of greasy hemp;

A vacant shoe, an empty tie, a ripped shirt,
   a lonely hat, and a pair of trousers stiff
   with black blood.
And upon the trampled grass were buttons, dead
   matches, butt-ends of cigars and cigarettes,
   peanut shells, a drained gin-flask, and a
   whore's lipstick [.]

It was inevitable, as *Native Son* would show us a few years later, that such white violence against black should be met by black violence against white.

The Marxist view of life was to be found in every poem Wright published in the 1930's. Once the Thirties were over, he all but stopped writing poetry. He may have come to understand that his greatest strength lay in poetical prose rather than in poetry itself.

Communists saw a crude but effectively propagandistic power in Wright's poetry, and they were even more pleased with his prose of social protest. From their point of view, one of his best articles was "Joe Louis Uncovers Dynamite."[9]

When Joe Louis defeated Max Baer and became boxing's heavyweight champion of the world, impoverished black ghettoes across the country rocked with joy and pride. Wright's article pleased the Communists because it linked black pride with the promises of the Communist Party. "Say, Comrade, here's the wild river that's got to be harnessed and directed. Here's *something,* that pent-up folk consciousness. . . . Here's that fluid something that's like iron. Here's the real dynamite that Joe Louis uncovered!" Then Wright punched home another article on Joe Louis, on the Louis-Schmelling fight, "High Tide in Harlem: Joe Louis as a Symbol of Freedom."[10]

Before leaving Chicago for the even more militantly leftist challenge of New York, Wright saw his third story published, "Big Boy Leaves Home."[11] The story shows how a carefree black boy can have his childhood cut short by the white world. As in most of Wright's later stories and novels, there is a basic concern with childhood and children's perception of reality, with the fear and violence that blur the fine line between reality and illusion, with flight from a white man's law, and with the imagery of fire and darkness.

Big Boy and three of his friends have cut school to enjoy a beautiful, sunny day. They clown and horse around through the wooded southern countryside. Someone lets a strong fart and they collapse in adolescent laughter. It's a warm day so they decide to swim bare-assed in a creek, though it means trespassing on a white man's land.

Wright draws a pastoral scene composed of a butterfly at the creek's edge, a droning bee, the scent of honeysuckle, sparrows in the woods, and the boys sunning themselves and chewing on blades of grass. Suddenly a white woman appears. The pastoral peace destroyed, the black boys make a panicked effort to get their scattered clothes without being seen. They know what can happen to a black man or child as a result of such "contact" with a white woman. The woman does see them and screams. Her male companion comes into view with a rifle and without a word begins firing. Two of the four boys are killed. Big Boy wrestles the rifle away and accidentally kills the white man. Both Big Boy and his surviving friend, Bobo, must take flight, leaving their childhood games behind forever.

From his hiding place in a small cave, Big Boy is agonized to see a lynch mob approaching with Bobo. Powerless to help, Big Boy watches Bobo being tortured, tarred and set afire. Wright's imagery emphasizes the ghastliness of whiteness as a destructive force against blackness. "[H]e saw a writhing white mass cradled in yellow flame, and heard screams, one on top of the other, each shriller and shorter than the last."

Big Boy turns from this scene unwilling to believe what his eyes have seen. He has the sensation that he has been dreaming, that the whole terrible experience he has gone through is somehow unreal. No longer a child, sobered by his sudden sense of maturity and the full awareness of his blackness, Big Boy hitchhikes north, shaking off his roots, hoping that in going north he will find something better.

Did Wright exaggerate his description of the lynching in "Big Boy Leaves Home"? Was he writing from an overactive imagination prodded by hearsay?

When he was nine years old and living in Memphis, one of several towns to which his mother took him to live while she sought work or tried to regain her health, Wright witnessed the aftermath of violence. A Negro had been lynched outside the city limits by a mob of 5,000, burned alive, his heart cut out, and his body dismembered. The man's head and one of his legs "were propped up on Beale Street and a white barbershop sought to attract customers by a souvenir of the body."[12] Wright lived on Beale Street.

Some of the fiction Wright wrote during his Chicago period was not published at the time. *Lawd Today,* an early novel, finally appeared in 1963, three years after the author's death. It is important as an experimental novel that shows Wright's growing control and power. Like James Joyce in *Ulysses* (which he may have read), Wright restricts the action of his 189-page novel to the classical unity of a twenty-four hour period, drawing out in that time span the major elements of his protagonist's life. Wright seemed to be trying to mold a character who is a black version of Joyce's Leopold Bloom.

Just as Joyce's Leopold Bloom is an outsider, a Jew in Catholic Ireland, so too is Wright's Jake Jackson an outsider, a Negro in White America. Both are nagged by wives who do not understand them, both are bothered by self-doubts and the taunts of "the others," both are anxious to experience life deeply enough to find it meaningful, and both are boxed in by circumstances. In the twenty-four hours described in each book, Jackson and Bloom visit bars with friends, lust after prostitutes, and dream about their desires. But Leopold Bloom keeps his frustration within himself, while Jake Jackson's frustration carries him into physical violence.

Jake Jackson works as a postal clerk in Chicago, a job that Richard Wright himself had found to be machine-like, mechanical, subhuman. In Jake Jackson's twenty-four hours he releases his pent-up frustrations through physical brutality against a scapegoat, his long-suffering and long-complaining wife; he gambles, drinks, and wenches—alternately dreaming and forgetting. Most of what we learn about him comes from his unspoken thoughts, also a chief source of character information in Wright's later fiction.

The three parts of the book are preceded by epigraphs appropriate to the aims of Wright's novel. These quotations are from Van Wyck Brooks's *America's Coming-of-Age,* Waldo Frank's *Our America,* and T. S. Eliot's *The Waste Land.* What Joyce had done in *Ulysses* and what Wright may have tried to do in *Lawd Today,* on a much smaller scale, was to recreate the inner world of a man's mind, to depict, as Wright's quotation from Van Wyck Brooks implies, ". . . a vast Sargasso

Sea—a prodigious welter of unconscious life, swept by groundswells of half-conscious emotion. . . ."

The three sections of *Lawd Today* are further prefaced by an excerpt from a fictional Lincoln's Day radio broadcast eulogizing Lincoln and recalling three moments in his noble life: his birth, the difficult Civil War period, and his assassination. Each fragment of the broadcast can be seen as a counterbalance or foil to a section of the novel, and each section of the novel as one of three moments in the ignoble life of Jake Jackson.

After an excerpt from the broadcast that speaks of the beautiful, breezy, peaceful day on which Americans are remembering Lincoln's birthday, Wright responds with "Commonplace," the first section of his novel. Compared to what will happen to Jake in later sections, this is a relatively calm part of his day and his life. After the broadcast excerpt about a critical point in the Civil War that was the most difficult moment in Lincoln's life, Wright's response is the second section of the novel, "Squirrel Cage." After the radio describes Lincoln's assassination, we are given the last section of the novel, "Rats' Alley." This part, like the assassination of Lincoln, is swift and abrupt.

Jake's story ends where it had started: with a complaining wife he can use as a scapegoat, and with the deadening routine of a wasted life. Jake's name probably was a modification of the name Jack Johnson —a Negro who fought against a deadening life and succeeded in becoming the first black heavyweight boxing champion of the world (1908). Jake Jackson does not experience the successful rise of a Lincoln or a Jack Johnson: he experiences only the daily assassinations of the stymied.

Lawd Today is expert enough in its techniques and

profound enough in the truths it presents to have mer-
ited immediate publication; instead, it had to wait almost thirty years. The Communist press was appar-
ently not interested in the book because it did not
openly stress any Marxist principles, and Wright was
still comparatively unknown by the establishment or
mainstream press.

By the time Wright moved to New York in May
1937, to become the Harlem editor of the official Communist newspaper, the *Daily Worker,* he was already a
skilled writer and moving closer to the fame that would
soon be his.

2

New York
(1937-1947)

Within days of his arrival in New York Wright was working with two prominent black Communists, James Ford and Benjamin Davis, Jr., both members of the Central Committee of the Communist Party. Davis asked Wright if in addition to serving as Harlem editor of the *Daily Worker* he would help edit a new literary quarterly, *New Challenge*. The emphasis of the periodical was to be upon Negro writers and the problems they face. Wright accepted.

To define and explain the objectives of *New Challenge* to other black writers, Wright composed a far-reaching article, "Blueprint for Negro Literature." Here he spoke of the value and function of Negro folklore, Black Nationalism, Marxism, and art as a weapon for changing the structure of society. It was important, said Wright, that the black writer not isolate himself: he must work as part of a collective power, neither forsaking professional autonomy nor forgetting the strength that comes from a united effort.[1]

Wright tried hard to follow his own advice. He sought to strike a difficult balance between professional autonomy and the larger social causes he knew his writing could assist. Restrained by a minimum of Party control over his fiction, he continued to write short stories. One, "Fire and Cloud,"[2] won a *Story* magazine prize (1938). For a Federal Writers' Project, *New York City Guide* (1939), he wrote a survey-essay, "Negroes in Manhattan." And for the Party he wrote articles setting forth its official positions on such political matters as support of the Loyalists against Franco Fascism in the Spanish Civil War; involvement of Negroes in the class struggle; neutrality, and later, after the Germans broke their nonaggression pact with the USSR (invading Russia on June 22, 1941), support of the war effort against Nazi Germany.

As a result of all the confusing twists and turns in Communist tactics and positions, Wright found himself growing disillusioned, not with Marxist ideology, but with the petty and ruthless men who ran the Communist parties of the world. Yet as long as the Party did not interfere with his fiction-writing, he was reasonably content to endure the uncertain ideological winds.

In 1938, *Uncle Tom's Children,* Wright's first collection of fiction, was published, not by the leftist press with its limited audience, but by a prominent mainstream publisher, Harper and Brothers.

The collection of stories included "Big Boy Leaves Home," "Down by the Riverside," "Long Black Song," and "Fire and Cloud." A second edition (1940) added a fifth story, "Bright and Morning Star," and as a preface, the autobiographical essay "The Ethics of Living Jim Crow." All these stories had as their theme the maturation of a black man or woman moving, or struggling to move, from childlike naiveté to ripened militancy.

"Big Boy Leaves Home" shows a youth forced to escape the South; "Down by the Riverside," a man futilely struggling against the whirlpool of chance, uncontrollable circumstance; "Long Black Song," a young mother trying to recapture the innocence and purity of a past love; "Fire and Cloud," a minister vacillating between submission to the white power structure's wishes and the demonstrations that may bring much-needed assistance to his people (choosing the more courageous alternative); "Bright and Morning Star," an older mother in conflict between traditionally passive religion and the aggressive religion of Communism for which her son fought and gave his life (choosing to sacrifice her own life for her son's beliefs though she cannot completely accept them). One escape, one defeat, one draw, and two moral victories, in that order.

The most interesting of these five stories may be "the draw"—"Long Black Song." The main character, Sarah, cannot escape the past. She is a child clinging to childhood and the memory of the man she had loved. Silas, Sarah's husband, is a proud man, proud to own his little farm and be independent of white control. When Sarah meets a young white traveling salesman, her imagination, spurred on by the hypnotic music of the combination clock-phonograph he tries to sell, allows her to see in him the young black man she had loved, and his helpless demeanor seems to make him an extension of her baby. She allows him to make love to her. "She smiled. The white man was just like a little boy. Jus like a chile." The music of a Negro spiritual sends Sarah into a deep trance in which time is stopped. She translates religious fervor into sexual ecstasy, both feelings capable of bringing temporary liberation. The song and the salesman-made-child-and-lover take her through the emotions of a spiritual and sexual climax.

When the trumpet of the Lord shall sound . . .

She rose on circling waves of white bright days and dark black nights.

. . . and time shall be no more . . .

Higher and higher she mounted.

And the morning breaks . . .

Earth fell far behind, forgotten.

. . . eternal, bright and *fair . . .*

Echo after echo sounded.

When the saved of the earth shall gather . . .

Her blood surged like the long gladness of summer.

. . . over the other shore . . .

Her blood ebbed like the deep dream of sleep in winter.

And when the roll is called up yonder . . .

She gave up, holding her breath.

I'll be there . . .

A lump filled her throat. She leaned her back against a post, trembling, feeling the rise and fall of days and nights, of summer and winter; surging, ebbing, leaping about her, beyond her, far out over the fields to where earth and sky lay folded in darkness. She wanted to lie down and sleep, or else leap up and shout. When the music stopped she felt herself coming back, being let down slowly.

The words of the spiritual and of the narrative line that alternates with each verse of the song combine to make one unified song of its own, very much in the vein of the rhythmical prayers of Negro prayer-meetings in which each line of the minister's animated exhortation is met by an equally animated and impromptu response from the congregation.

Silas learns of this violation of his marital rights and kills the salesman; he then chooses to die fighting rather than be captured by white lawmen. Though Sarah is the focal point of the story, surrounded by music and the poetry of Wright's musical and soft-spoken language, the ending abruptly switches the focus to her husband. Sarah fails to see clearly, while Silas can claim a moral victory. One defeat balanced by one victory equals a draw.

Characteristic of most of Wright's fiction is the
sudden movement from extended lyricism, peaceful,
beautiful tableaux of nature and dreamily pleasant
musings, to bone-breaking scenes of violence. In this
respect, *Native Son* is like "Big Boy Leaves Home" and
"Long Black Song."

Two stories in the *Uncle Tom's Children* collection, "Fire and Cloud" and "Bright and Morning Star,"
contain the first important uses of Communism as a
subject for Wright's fiction, a theme that *Native Son*
would include. "Fire and Cloud" takes place in a southern city of 25,000 people, 10,000 of them black. The
city is suffering a famine and—predictably—the black
population is hardest hit. A dictatorial mayor, an im-
petuous chief of police (of the "don't-take-any-crap"
school), and a supercilious representative of the white
business establishment seek to head off what their intelligence reports indicate is a demonstration organized by
Communists. To enlist the help of a man they consider
an obedient Uncle Tom, the three city leaders call upon
the Reverend Dan Taylor, a Negro clergyman trusted
and respected by both black and white.

Because he foresees the strong possibility of violence, Taylor's dilemma is whether to counsel his people against demonstrating for the food they need, or to
counsel them to stand up for their rights and risk violence in a cause he knows is just.

His dilemma is complicated by his profound belief in the God of Christianity: his religion has taught
him how to endure but not how to overcome injustice.
He leads a prayer-meeting that places complete faith in
God. In Wright's excellently recreated minister's prayer
and congregational response, Reverend Taylor cries out
to the Lord,

"Lawd Gawd Awmighty, Yuh made the sun n the moon n the stars n the earth n the seas n mankind n the beasts of the fiels!"

yes jesus

"Yuh made em all, Lawd, n Yuh tol em whut t do!"

yuh made em lawd

"Yuhs strong n powerful n Yo will rules this worl!"

yuh rules it lawd

"Yuh brought the chillun of Israel outta the lan of Egypt!"

yuh sho did

"Yuh made the dry bones rise up outta the valley of death n live!"

yuh made em live lawd

"Yuh saved the Hebrew chillun in the fiery furnace!"

yes jesus

"Yuh stopped the storm n Yuh made the sun stan still!"

yuh stopped it lawd

"Yuh knocked down the walls of Jericho n Yuh kept Jona in the belly of the whale!"

yuh kept im lawd

"Yuh let Yo son Jesus walk on watah n Yuh brought Im back from the dead!"

have mercy jesus

"Yuh made the lame walk!"

yuh did it lawd

"Yuh made the blin see!"

help us now lawd

"Yuh made the deaf hear!"

glory t the mos high

"Lawd, Yuhs a rock in the tima trouble n Yuhs a shelter in the tima storm!"

he is he is

"Lawd, Yuh said Yuhd strike down the wicked men who plagued Yo chillun!"

glory to gawd

"Yuh said Yuhd destroy this ol worl n create a new Heaven n a new Earth!"

wes waitin on yuh jesus

"Lawd, Yuh said call on Yo name n Yuhd answer!"

yuh said it lawd n now wes callin

"Yuh made us n put the breatha life in us!"

yuh did lawd

"Now look down on us, Lawd! Speak t our hearts n let us know what Yo will is! Speak t us like Yuh spoke t Jacob!"

speak lawd n our souls will be clay in yo hans . . .

A man of God, Taylor is afraid to provoke violence. When he himself is whipped and beaten by white rabble, the only violence he is not afraid to provoke is the violence of God, which he calls down upon his tormentors. His back burning from the beating, he walks "[l]ike a pillar of fire," invoking God's wrath: "Some days theys gonna burn in Gawd Awmightys fire! How come they make us suffer so? Gawd, ef yuh gimme the strength Ahll tear this ol buildin down! Tear it down, Lawd! Tear it down like ol Samson tore the temple down!"

Opposed to Taylor is the hysterical deacon of his church, Deacon Smith—outspoken, insulting, and jealous of Taylor's popularity. He is unalterably opposed to Negro participation in a demonstration, because he fears violence and because he wants absolutely no contact with Communists, not even in a common, just cause. Taylor, however, is not much disturbed by the fact that Communists are involved in the proposed demonstration. It is the new, alien way of attempting a change that bothers him—direct confrontation with white power. His religion has not prepared him for such an eventuality, and an endorsement of the demonstration strikes him as a break with traditional faith.

While Deacon Smith cannot change, Taylor can. Partly inspired by his questioning, restless son, and partly convinced by the arguments of the Communists, he does change, coming to a new resolution and a new recognition. His resolution is to stop being passive and to speak up for what he believes, even if his newly expressed inner thoughts may result in further physical abuse or even death. His recognition is that all blacks must stand together: he sees this unity as even more important than the support that will come from the Communists. When toward the end of the story his son, Jimmy, says "Them Reds wuz right," Taylor replies, with a far less than full commitment to Communism "Ah dunno . . . But let nothin come between yuh n *yo* people. Even the Reds cant do nothin ef yuh lose yo people."

For a traditional Negro clergyman, Dan Taylor has undergone a significantly drastic revolution. He sees that faith in God is no longer enough. The old religion is no longer valid, he tells his son. As a minister to his people he must also stand with them and have faith in them. God is not an abstraction to be prayed to stoically, but a part of the people—and the people must act.

When the demonstration takes place, the establishment's power is overwhelmed. As the Communists had predicted, the poor whites join forces with the blacks. Taylor reaffirms the existence of God, but he immediately follows his reaffirmation with a cry of militancy: *"Freedom belongs t the strong!"* Wright underscores this cry with italics.

In "Bright and Morning Star"[3] Wright continues to explore the evolution of black religion from its traditional forms of expression to a militant weapon. Aunt Sue, the story's central character, had watched her two sons rebel against the attitude of sufferance and for-

bearance taught by the "Old Negro," by Negroes like
Deacon Smith and, initially, Reverend Taylor. With one
of her sons already in jail and all hope lost for his release, Aunt Sue throws herself as wholeheartedly as she
can behind the Communist ideology to which her remaining son, Johnny-Boy, is so devoted. The past and
the present become mixed in her, grating against one
another: she becomes caught in the ambiguously gray
world of semilight, between the old evening star of
Christianity and the new, brighter, morning star of
Communism. When she recalls the traditional spirituals,
even their meaning is unclear. She sings, *"Hes the Lily
of the Valley, the Bright n Mawnin Star,"* and she is
moved uncertainly, vacillating between the old meta-
phorical, symbolic meanings and the new.

Johnny-Boy is idealistic. He makes no distinction
between white and black in Communist ranks. When
someone tips off the rural Tennessee policemen that the
Communists are planning a meeting, Aunt Sue assumes,
correctly, that there must be a white informer in the
Party's ranks. Johnny-Boy insists that white and black
comrades are merely poor people who must stand together in complete trust. His mother trusts only one
white person, Reva, a girl who is in love with Johnny-
Boy. It is Reva who—to express her identification with
the black family—calls the Negro mother Aunt Sue.

When the planned meeting of Communists is
threatened by a police invasion, Johnny-Boy sloshes
through mud and rain to warn members not to attend.
Though the police beat Aunt Sue, with stubborn courage she refuses to give them the names of the Communists. While she is still stunned from the beating,
Booker, a new white member of the Party, enters and
comforts her. At first Aunt Sue sees him as "a vast
white blur," like a face in an ambiguous dream, but her

vision slowly clears. Pretending that he wants to help Johnny-Boy, whom he says the police have captured, Booker asks her for the names of all the Party members. Despite her instinctual suspicion that Booker is the informer, she gives him the names.

The rest of the story shows Aunt Sue determined to prevent the informer from using this treacherously obtained information. Hiding Johnny-Boy's gun under a white sheet, she hurries to the wooded hillside where her son is being interrogated. "The sheriff tol me t bring a sheet t git his body," she tells the white men. She stalls for time until Booker arrives. For her entertainment the men torture Johnny-Boy, breaking his legs, then his eardrums. Booker shows up and Aunt Sue kills him before he can reveal names. The sheriff's mob shoots Johnny-Boy and then Aunt Sue. Pushed beyond the ambiguous gray of indecision by the white violence against a black dream, she had, however, finally accepted the new "bright morning star."

Throughout the story Wright alludes to a cold white mountain. To Aunt Sue that white mountain was "the white folks and their laws" and it was "temptation, something to lure her from her Lord, a part of the world God had made in order that she might endure it and come through all the stronger." The hardships she had endured without attacking the white mountain had once tested and strengthened her faith in Christ, but her sons had pulled her away from traditional Christianity, replacing its images with new ones. In the new religion, Communism, the mountain was something to be conquered, not endured.

So firmly rooted in Communist idealism was "Bright and Morning Star," and so firmly committed to Communism was Wright at this moment, that he was anxious to use the story to assist the Communist movement. In 1941 he therefore permitted the Marxist house, International Publishers, to reissue the story as a separate volume that included a special preface entitled "A Letter to International Publishers."

In that letter Wright asks that the royalties from the publication be used for the defense of Earl Browder, the Kansas-born general secretary of the Communist Party of the United States. Browder had been convicted in 1940 of misusing a passport in 1934, and he had been sentenced to four years in prison. When Richard Wright wrote his letter, the Browder conviction was on appeal to the United States Supreme Court. The Court upheld the conviction and Browder began to serve his term, but in May 1941 the sentence was commuted by President Roosevelt. Browder retained his position as Party leader until he was toppled from power in 1945.

I am glad to be able to assign to International Publishers the reprint rights to "Bright and Morning Star." Frankly, it is not my story; it belongs to the workers. I would never have written it unless I had felt that I had a workers' audience to read it. Ever since it was first published in the pages of the *New Masses* some two years ago, I've wanted to see it published alone and cheaply enough for workers to buy and read. . . .

"Down by the Riverside," the final story in the *Uncle Tom's Children* collection, is both stylistically and ideologically less intricate. It focuses on Brother Mann, whose wife has been unable to give birth after four agonizing days of labor. Because the southern town is flooded by heavy rains and broken levees, he cannot obtain medical attention for her. He knows that no white man, in this time of flooding, is likely to go out of his way to help a Negro in distress. His only hope,

as he sees it, is to find a boat and take his wife to the
Red Cross Hospital. A friend steals a boat from Heartfield, an old white man who hates Negroes. Mann rows
down the river, gets lost, and by a tragic coincidence
winds up in front of Heartfield's house. The white man
spots the boat, attempts to shoot Mann, and is himself
killed in the ensuing struggle. Badly frightened, Mann
continues on his way, but he arrives at the hospital too
late—his wife is dead.

Now both Mann and the stolen boat are con-
scripted to aid in the reinforcement of the remaining
levees and the evacuation of trapped white people. By
another great coincidence two survivors he stops for in
the dark turn out to be Heartfield's wife and child. He is
recognized as the old man's killer. At this point Mann
could have chosen to flee and let the wife and child
die, but paralyzed by fatalism he rescues them, thus as-
suring his own death. He begins to study himself and
his surroundings with the objective detachment of a
nonparticipating observer. As he had feared, the woman
and child tell rescue workers that he had killed Heartfield. Mann is shot and killed.

Two very brief stories not included in either edition of *Uncle Tom's Children* but written in the 1930's
were "Silt" and "Almos' a Man." First published in
1937,[4] "Silt" was reprinted in Wright's later collection
of short stories, *Eight Men* (1961), under the title "The
Man Who Saw the Flood." It is little more than a brief
anecdote of a southern rural Negro family returning to
a mud-caked, damaged home after a flood. They clean
up, resigned to remaining despite hopelessly high debts.
The thought of fleeing without paying the debts is re-
jected because "The'll put us in jail." "Almos' a Man,"
a more effective anecdote story, was published in January 1940[5] and reprinted in *Eight Men* as "The Man

Who Was Almost a Man." It is a poignant depiction of
a child seeking a foothold in the world of adults. Dave
Saunders, a seventeen-year-old black boy living in the
rural south, begs his mother for two dollars from his
own farm wages to buy an old gun at a general store.
On the border of adulthood, he yearns to be respected
as a man and he wants to feel a sense of power over
other men. A gun, he naively thinks, will be all he needs
to achieve respect and power. Practicing, he accidentally
kills a farmer's mule. Vainly he tries to fill a gaping
hole in the side of the mule with mud. But mud will not
revive a dead mule and Dave is faced with a fifty-dollar
debt: two dollars a month for two years. He jumps a
freight train, going away "to somewhere where he
could be a man."

Not long after the first publication of *Uncle Tom's
Children,* Wright received a Guggenheim Fellowship
that helped him complete work on *Native Son.* This
award came in the year 1939, the same year in which
he became a married man. With Ralph Ellison as his
best man, he married Rose Dhima Meadman, a Rus-
sian-American dancer who had a cosmopolitan knowledge of many countries, including the Soviet Union,
where she, and her mother before her, had once danced.

When in March 1940 Harper published *Native
Son,* Richard and Dhima were overwhelmed by the
publicity as the sales of the novel soared. After slightly
more than one month, sales totaled a quarter of a million copies. According to Cass Canfield, Harper's executive editor, *Native Son* sales were off to a better start
than any other Harper novel in twenty years.[6] The
Book-of-the-Month Club chose the book as its March
selection. Within a year Wright was awarded the Spingarn Medal, given annually to an American Negro for
high achievement. A few months later Wright was again

honored, this time at a gathering of Marxist writers, the fourth biannual American Writers Congress.

Despite the almost universal acclaim from the mainstream and the Marxist left, *Native Son* found its influential detractors. Some mainstream critics considered the book's credibility damaged by excesses of hatred and violence, which they felt were not at all representative of Negroes in America. A portion of the Marxist left found too much emphasis on an individual Negro's rebellion and not enough of an appeal for constructive group action.

Few novels open more strikingly and startlingly than *Native Son*. A rat is smashed to death in a slum tenement on Chicago's south side. As Bigger Thomas, age 20, wakes up one dark morning to the insistent ringing of an alarm clock, his sleepy eyes focus upon a large rat. With hatred, disgust and fear mixed in him, Bigger kills the ugly rodent, crushing it with all his might. The violent death of the rat, symbol of the economic forces that oppress the poor, foreshadows Bigger's violent efforts to break out of the physical and mental rattrap his life has been. With his mother, younger brother and sister, he had come North—like Richard Wright, from Jackson, Mississippi—hoping to break the tragic cycle of his life in the South. What he found was continuing enslavement.

The first section of the novel is entitled "Fear." Bigger cannot accept himself as an individual; he is afraid to face his emotions. He hates the white man for making him feel inferior and hate himself. He lives in a constant shuttle between positive self-assertion and damaging self-condemnation.

Behind Bigger's vacillating emotions there is a force he cannot comprehend. "These were the rhythms of his life: indifference and violence; periods of abstract

brooding and periods of intense desire; moments of silence and moments of anger—like water ebbing and
flowing from the tug of a far-away, invisible force. . . .
He was like a strange plant blooming in the day and
wilting at night; but the sun that made it bloom and the
cold darkness that made it wilt were never seen. It was
his own sun and darkness, a private and personal sun
and darkness."[7]

Bigger goes to a double feature movie. Both films
aggravate or feed his self-doubt. One, *The Gay Woman,*
depicts white men and women strolling on beaches and
dancing in nightclubs. The other, *Trader Horn,* shows
black men and women doing savage dances against the
background of the jungle. The white world around him
strikes Bigger as being as unreal as the white world of
The Gay Woman. He still lacks the courage to intrude
upon such a world.

A relief agency finds Bigger a job as chauffeur to
a wealthy white family, the Daltons. His fear of walking
through a white section of the city makes him take
weapons when he goes for the interview. "He was going
among white people, so he would take his knife and his
gun; it would make him feel that he was the equal of
them, give him a sense of completeness."[8] He goes to
the Dalton home determined to act as he thinks a white
employer expects a Negro to act.

Henry Dalton is simultaneously a slum landlord—
it later is confirmed that his real estate company owns
the Thomases' rat-infested building—and a supporter of
the NAACP, contributing ping-pong tables instead of
decent housing.

Mary, Mr. Dalton's naive college-student daughter,
tries, without the slightest understanding, to be a radical like Jan Erlone, her Communist friend. Together
Mary and Jan befriend Bigger. Suspiciously, Bigger

senses that Mary treats him as a pet, and Jan, though more aware of Bigger's fears and needs, simply puzzles him. Jan's openness doesn't fit in with the sinister picture of slinking, shadowy monsters American newspapers portray Communists as being.

On his first night as chauffeur, Bigger is coaxed to drink with Mary and Jan. Mary gets very drunk and Bigger takes her home, lugs her up the stairs to her bedroom, and plops her down. Himself a bit loosened by drink, he allows his hand to brush against her body, touches her breasts, kisses her lips, and as she responds positively, kisses her again.

Suddenly the bedroom door creaks open and Bigger is in the position of a Big Boy who has to leave home. Mary's mother stands at the door. Robed in white she seems to be a white blur, silent and ghostlike. She is blind, but her eyes pierce the air, abetted by the eyes of the white cat that follows her. The deeply-engrained taboo against a black man's contact with a white woman creates in Bigger an overwhelming fear of lynching. He panics. In an effort to silence Mary's mumbling he presses a pillow against her mouth. Mrs. Dalton leaves. The pillow is removed. Mary is dead.

Though not comprehending what has happened, Bigger still has the presence of mind to dispose of the body. He stuffs it into a trunk, carries the trunk on his back, and tries to stuff the body into the basement furnace. Because the body won't go easily into the furnace he hacks off the head, using both knife and hatchet.

Wright spares no detail. He wants the reader to be as revolted by black violence as by white violence, and to understand the social conditions responsible. "[Bigger] touched the sharp blade to the throat, just touched it as if expecting the knife to cut the white flesh of itself . . . Gently, he sawed the blade into the flesh and struck a bone. . . . He whacked at the bone with the knife. The head hung limply on the newspapers, the curly black hair dragging about in blood. He whacked harder, but the head would not come off. . . . He got the hatchet . . ."⁹ For the first time in his life Bigger impinges meaningfully on the white world. He has a fleeting sense of power and freedom.

Book II, "Flight," begins as Book I had begun, with Bigger in bed, awakening to the consciousness of the run-down bleak apartment which held him prisoner.

Bigger tries to get $10,000 in ransom money from the Daltons by making it appear that Jan Erlone or other Communists had kidnapped Mary. His black girl friend, Bessie, is forced to help him.

Newspaper headlines blazon the arrest of Jan and the plan seems to be working until a newspaper reporter finds human bones in the furnace. Bigger panics and flees with Bessie.

Holed up in a freezing and deserted South Side slum tenement, Bigger knows from a newspaper he steals that the police are closing in on him. Nevertheless, he experiences a giddy sense of intoxication, of personal worth, even of pleasure. His acts against the Daltons, combined with the newspaper headlines, have given him a firmer identity, proof of existence. In celebration he forces Bessie to have sexual intercourse. Satisfied physically but sleepless, Bigger now asks himself what he can do with Bessie. It would be hard to run with her and he couldn't leave her behind to talk. As she sleeps he bludgeons her with a brick and throws her body out the window. "He lifted the brick again and again, until in falling it struck a sodden mass that gave softly but stoutly to each landing blow. Soon he seemed to be striking a wet wad of cotton, of some damp substance whose only life was the jarring of the brick's impact."[10] Not long afterward the police trap him on a rooftop and he is captured.

Why does Wright make his protagonist so unheroic, so cruel? In the essay "How 'Bigger' Was Born," Wright supplies an answer. "I had written a book [*Uncle Tom's Children*] which even bankers' daughters could read and weep over and feel good. I swore to myself that if I ever wrote another book, no one would weep over it; that it would be so hard and deep that they would have to face it without the consolation of tears."[11] Bigger Thomas is a character who, having been destroyed, destroys others.

Book III, "Fate," shows Bigger in prison: awaiting trial, undergoing the trial, and, having been condemned to die in the electric chair, awaiting execution. Whatever narrative there is in the novel ends with Book II. The last third of *Native Son* is really an analysis of the first two-thirds.

During his first days in prison Bigger asks for a newspaper. He wants to read about himself. He is still not sure of who or what he is, and the newspaper gives him an unambiguous identity, one imposed from outside. It tells him he is a rapist (of Mary), not an alleged rapist, that he resembles an ape, and that he is an inhuman object without heart or compassion. Included in the newspaper article is a biographical sketch of Bigger's childhood in Jackson. The article says Bigger came from a shiftless, immoral family, that he was at an early age an incorrigible criminal; it implies that God should have punished him with a death penalty long ago.

The pastor of his mother's church visits Bigger. Asking him to think of eternal life, he reads to him from Genesis. But Bigger had killed the picture of Creation in his mind long before he had killed Mary. That had been his first murder, Mary his second, and Bessie his third. Excluded from life, Bigger had killed both God and Man. All that was left was a black void to be filled with nothing positive. His life, momentarily concrete and substantial with the feel of "white" blood, has slipped back into the flimsy realm of a sick mind haunted by ghosts and apparitions of Mrs. Dalton. The pastor does nothing for Bigger but bring back a picture of all these murders, a picture dancing in his head and walking "before his eyes like a ghost in the night, creating within him a sense of exclusion that was as cold as a block of ice."[12]

Jan Erlone, whom Bigger had tried to frame for Mary's death, visits Bigger's cell, awkward and nervous over how to tell a black man that a white man can feel closer to him than to other white men. Jan is portrayed in this scene as obviously open-hearted and sincere. In his openness, his forgiveness for a frame-up that could have cost him his life, and his forgiveness for the murder of the girl he loved, Jan has passed the test of fire—guilty till proved innocent of racism. For the first time in his life Bigger sees Jan, or any other white man, not as part of a threatening white mass, but as a person.

At the grand jury hearings the prosecution surprises defense counsel with what one would think is inadmissible evidence—Bessie's body is carted into the courtroom. Bigger had already signed a confession admitting the accidental killing of Mary, and the murder of Bessie. The defense strategy was to plead guilty but to attempt to prove extenuating circumstances, thereby reducing the charge to manslaughter or second-degree murder. Bigger sees that the court is not concerned with the killing of a black woman but only with using her as "evidence" that he had raped and killed Mary in the same manner.

Bigger understands that it is essentially for the murder of a white woman, Mary Dalton, that he must be punished. "[H]e knew that the white people did not really care about Bessie's being killed. White people never searched for Negroes who killed other Negroes. He had even heard it said that white people felt it was good when one Negro killed another; it meant that they had one Negro less to contend with. Crime for a Negro was only when he harmed whites, took white lives, or injured white property."[13]

Wright would have understood, in the race riots of the late 1960's, how white people would react with horror at the destruction of white-owned property while paying scant attention to the Negroes shot and killed by the police. He was trying to explain these dangerous values that later writers would re-examine.

The emotions aroused in court by the display of Bessie's body spill over into the city. As the police lead him through a street, Bigger sees an angry white mob burning a cross and calling for his fiery death. Thoughts of the Ku Klux Klan blend with the wooden cross of Christ that his mother's minister had placed around his neck, and when he is returned to a cell he angrily tears the cross from his throat.

Defense counsel for Bigger is Jan's friend Boris A. Max, a Jewish lawyer from the Labor Defenders, a Communist-affiliated group. In his private questioning of Bigger, Max provides the sounding board for Bigger's self-exploration, *i.e.,* Wright speaking about sociological conditions and resulting psychological reactions.

At the trial itself Bigger feels he's living out "a wild and intense dream that must end soon, somehow." Max—whom Bigger always addresses as Mr. Max—feels that the court is not willing to consider evidence that could mitigate Bigger's punishment. Max cites as a precedent the Leopold-Loeb case in which rich white boys who were clearly guilty of kidnapping and first-degree murder, escaped the death penalty. But the lawyer sees that Bigger has no fair chance in this bigoted climate.

Wright devotes sixteen pages to Max's defense summation. This section is in essence an unabsorbed lump, an eloquent philosophical essay that would fit more easily into Wright's "How 'Bigger' Was Born" essay than into the novel. The temptation to impose heavy polemics upon his work is a carry-over from the many polemical essays of the 1930's and would continue to be characteristic of some of Wright's later fiction. This is especially true of *The Outsider* (1953), where we find a fifteen-page lecture on modern industrialization and its effect upon human life. This section would fit more easily into Wright's *White Man, Listen!* (1957), which does have an article entitled "Tradition and Industrialization."

The defense summation in *Native Son* indicts the society that allowed the development of a Bigger Thomas. Max's argument is careful not to restrict the problem to a racial one. It calls attention to the dangerous creation of two separate societies, one imprisoned within the other, "twelve million black people . . . a separate nation, stunted, stripped, and held captive *within* this nation, devoid of political, social, economic, and property rights."[14] But it also calls attention to governmental preference for manufacturers' associations in their disputes with workers and labor unions, to discrimination that has too often divided people into the influential rich and the overlooked poor.

What Max says in this summation is in large part what Wright also believes. But Max's commendable rational understanding does not carry over to an even more important emotional understanding. He can understand the causes of Bigger's anger, fear, and frustration, but he cannot begin to fathom the depths of emotion within a black man after he is pushed up against a wall.

Bigger does not hate all whites, nor does he stand as an isolated instance of black rebellion. He is an instrument of change and education in others. As he approaches what he knows will be the end of his life, he has a compulsion. He must convey the deepest and darkest secret within himself; he must reveal the meaning of his life. He must tell Max what Max does not understand—that the twilight, unclear world in which he has been forced to live was dangerously ambiguous, filled with shadows, play-acting, motion pictures, newspaper headlines, all elements of second-hand living, and that he could not grasp either himself or the world until he had killed. " 'What I killed for must've been good! . . . I didn't know I was really alive in this world until I felt things hard enough to kill for 'em.' "[15] The hard truth of these words is perhaps impossible for Max to understand. After these unexpected words "Max's eyes were full of terror." He hesitates, wanting to go to Bigger, but feeling powerless and speechless. His eyes wet, he says good-bye to Bigger, gropes "like a blind man" for his hat, and turns to leave, keeping his face averted from Bigger.

Although no white man in *Native Son* fully understands Bigger, the possibility of meaningful communication between the races is not blotted out. Bigger's last request of Max is to say hello to Jan. The exact words of the request are important: " 'Tell . . . Tell Mister . . . Tell Jan hello. . . .' "[16] Bigger is still not able to see himself as a brother or comrade on an equal footing with a white man, but the wall between his world and the white world develops a hopeful crack in it. Bigger still calls Boris Max by his last name, but, rather uncomfortably and hesitantly, he can bring himself to use Jan's first name.

When Bigger is executed for his crimes, he is formally killed by the society that had been slowly murdering him all his life. The sharp stabbing pain of the execution may, like his killing of others, for a split second confirm the fact that he does exist. Perhaps, however, the process of dying is merely a return to invisibility and to the blurred vision: the ambiguity of a reality inseparable from dreams that smile and dreams—nightmares—that frown.

Native Son showed not only Wright's power with fiction but also his temptation to lapse into essay-writing. In the five years after *Native Son*, Wright published three major works: *12 Million Black Voices* (1941), *The Man Who Lived Underground* (1944), and *Black Boy* (1945). The 1941 and 1945 works were nonfiction, each a book-length essay.

The outgrowth of a WPA project, *12 Million Black Voices: A Folk History of the Negro in the United States* is a sociological study of the Negro migration from the rural South to the urban North. Accompanied by photographs chosen by Edwin Rosskam from the files of the Farm Security Administration, Wright's text traces with poetic eloquence, as well as insight, the continuing bondage of black men, from slavery and plantation life to sharecropping on exhausted soil and, later, to the sweatshops of northern cities.

In choosing the title for this volume (as well as for *Black Boy* and *Black Power*), Wright makes a conscious point of picking the word "black" and not the word "Negro" (although the book's subtitle uses the word "Negro," perhaps as a synonym for "slave"). Wright feels that the use of the word "Negro" contributes to the black man's difficulty in establishing his identity and making contact with other Americans. Wright's point was made almost thirty years before the current revolt against the terms "Negro" and "colored." He says in *12 Million Black Voices* that "Negro" is a white man's word that does not describe; it is a "psychological island" that artificially limits the scope of a black man's life and helps set it apart from the lives of other Americans.[17]

The threads of black nationalism are strong in Wright's text for *12 Million Black Voices*, going far beyond the choice of "black" over "Negro." Wright speaks of African civilization as a culture that can inspire pride and give a sense of identification to its descendants. He rejects the commonly held belief that African culture was monolithic and monolithically primitive.

We had our own civilization in Africa before we were captured and carried off to this land. You may smile when we call the way of life we lived in Africa "civilization," but in numerous respects the culture of many of our tribes was equal to that of the lands from which the slave captors came. We smelted iron, danced, made music, and recited folk poems; we sculptured, worked in glass, spun cotton and wool, wove baskets and cloth; we invented a medium of exchange, mined silver and gold, made pottery and cutlery; we fashioned tools and utensils of brass, bronze, ivory, quartz, and granite; we had our own literature, our own systems of law, religion, medicine, science, and education; we painted in color upon rocks; we raised cattle, sheep, and goats; we planted and harvested grain—in short, centuries before the Romans ruled, we lived as men.[18]

Coupled with a strong current of black nationalism is an anti-Christian sentiment reminiscent of the struggle of dogmas in "Fire and Cloud" and "Bright and Morning Star." There the struggle was between Christianity and Communism. Here, and again in *Black Power*, the struggle is primarily between white imperialism, which can take the guise of Christianity to enforce its injustices, and black nationalism.

Wright speaks of the black African's "[c]aptivity under Christendom" as having "blasted" his life, destroying family life, traditions, and all values which had, in the Africa before the white man, given life meaning.[19] White men extended Christian salvation with one hand while denying freedom with the other. Even the prayers and hymns of the white man's religion that the black man adopted seemed to reinforce the bonds of slavery, says Wright. They taught that the suffering was ordained by God. Yet one of the few emotional releases open to blacks who feared the White God was the weekly prayer-meeting.[20]

12 Million Black Voices makes the point, from a Marxist perspective, that American society is based upon class distinctions and a concept of materialist success. The book also draws the Marxist conclusion that black and white workers must stand together in a united front against the classes that exploit them.[21] Wright finds three classes in America that stand above the vast majority of black men: the people who run the plantations (Wright calls them Lords of the Land), the people who run the industries (Wright calls them Bosses of the Buildings), and the poor white workers who compete with the blacks for bread. He speaks of five million landless poor white workers and four million landless poor black workers, both being cheated by the rural lords and the urban bosses, and forced to fight each other instead of uniting against their oppressors.

In addition to elements of black nationalism, anti-Christian sentiment, and Marxism, *12 Million Black Voices* contains Wright's omnipresent concern with dreams and nightmares. "We black men and women in America today, as we look back upon scenes of rapine, sacrifice, and death, seem to be children of a devilish aberration, descendants of an interval of nightmare in history, fledglings of a period of amnesia on the part of men who once dreamed a great dream and forgot."[22]

As *12 Million Black Voices* appeared in print, Wright completed a 150-page manuscript for a new novel. His agent had difficulty in getting it published: Harper and Brothers considered it too short to be issued as a novel, and several magazines were approached but declined.[23] Finally, in the spring of 1942, a new magazine, *Accent*, published about ten pages, as "Two Excerpts from a Novel."[24] Subsequently, the manuscript was drastically cut, and in its abridged form *The Man Who Lived Underground* appeared in Edwin Seaver's anthology *Cross Section 1944*.[25] The original version has never been published—an entire opening section of seventy typewritten pages was dropped[26]—and indeed there is no reason why it should be published, since the abridged version stands as an excellent work of art. It may well be Wright's best work. Its narrative is swift and compelling, uninterrupted by polemical impulses; its themes of invisibility and self-discovery are provocatively presented, enough to have influenced Ralph Ellison in the writing of *Invisible Man* (1952); and its use of imagery and symbols is as skillful and as representative of Wright's craftsmanship as any work one can choose.

The novelette tells the story of a black who, after being forced by the police to sign a confession to a crime he has not committed, escapes and hides in a sewer. In a cave jutting out from the sewer's stream he establishes a home, an existence of sorts, and from there he makes excursions through the basements of businesses, a motion picture theater, and a church. Wright dissects this character's psychological reactions to his restricted world and to his fleeting contacts with the above-surface world. The protagonist, who finds he must begin from a zero comprehension to piece together the confusing elements of his existence, seeking his identity in a blind, racist world, is unnamed by Wright until midway through the story. Slowly and hesitantly the man pecks out his name on a typewriter stolen along with other loot from the shops he has entered at night on his daily journeys through the sewers: "freddaniels." Later, back in his cave, having now learned how to make capital letters and spaces between words, he decides again to write his name but can no longer remember it. Nor can he remember why he had run from the police. For only one brief moment the invisible man had recalled his name, and the name is never mentioned or recalled a second time.

In the man's dream-like, nightmarish existence, or nonexistence, he sees much that is frightening. He sees a large rat baring its teeth at him, an ominous and threatening symbol, as in *Native Son*, of stagnation, disease, and death. The man's nostrils are attacked by the odor of rot, and his mind is attacked by the darkness and silence. Suddenly the silence is broken by the faint sound of church singing. Through a crevice he sees black men and women in white robes, singing. Stifling an initial impulse to laugh, his mood changes to one of disgust. Here are people singing while the stench of sewer air is everywhere. The whole religious experience of praying to God for something, for anything, strikes him as futile.

Continuing on his sewer river travels of discovery— a journey as bizarre as Marlow's trip up a Congo river in Conrad's *Heart of Darkness*—freddaniels sees a dead, naked baby floating by, and his reaction to the tiny corpse is the same as his reaction to the church prayers. "[I]t was dead, cold, nothing, the same nothingness he had felt while watching the men and women singing in the church. . . . The eyes were closed, as though in sleep; the fists were clenched, as though in protest; and the mouth gaped black in soundless cry."[27] The protagonist's reaction to this scene is essential—the recognition that he exists but without a clear sense of essence, of what defines him. Certainly the church cannot give him the definition he needs. Nor does there seem to be any other avenue out of an irrational, absurd universe. Wright had read Dostoyevsky, Camus, Sartre, and other existential writers, but such a philosophy was instinctive to a sensitive outsider like Richard Wright, and like freddaniels.

Climbing the celler steps of a funeral parlor the underground man sees an adult corpse and a glass container into which the body's blood has been drained, an embalming process to delay the inevitable rotting.

In the basement of a motion picture house he comes across a furnace and an exit sign, both glowing red and looking infernal. People in the theater are laughing at a film while this hell and sewer lie beneath them. Stoking the furnace is an old man who works without turning on the light. The protagonist realizes that the old man has adjusted to the dark world in which he lives.

Curiously enough, like the furnace stoker, freddaniels becomes attached to his other-world existence. It becomes a sort of womb, filled with comfort and security, lighted by electric bulbs he has wired, decorated with jewels and hundred-dollar bills stolen from stores he has visited at night.

The story's protagonist finally becomes aware that he cannot find happiness in the never-never land of the underground, that he cannot hope to find justice at the hands of white policemen above ground, that in spite of his innocence of the murder with which he is charged he bears a more fundamental guilt, and that he must communicate to someone his new-found understanding of a key fact of life. He sees that all men will steal and lie and be tempted to kill; he sees that all men are in some fundamental way guilty in their thoughts, their motives, and their deeds. He had watched as people whose common feeling of guilt found expression in prayer. He had watched as a businessman stole money from a safe, and a night watchman was beaten for it. "The watchman was guilty; although he was not guilty of the crime of which he had been accused, he was guilty, had always been guilty."[28]

When he tears himself away from his underground existence, freddaniels runs to the police with the compulsion to make a statement, to confess his guilt; he is not guilty of the crime of which he has been accused, but guilty in the deeper sense he has just discovered. But as he confronts the police, he can find no words adequate for the precise definitions he must communicate. Similarly incapable of articulating the arbitrarily assigned words that form his name, the only words he can now use are those of a child relating a dream or fairy tale. " 'It was a long time ago,' he spoke like a child relating a dimly remembered dream."[29]

The gulf between his thoughts and his words is too

wide, and the gulf between his thoughts and the comprehension of the police is immense. He appears to them insane, speaking like a child playing a child's game. In
his desperate need to communicate, he takes the police
to the sewer. When he climbs in and asks them to follow, he is shot down. "You've got to shoot his kind.
They'd wreck things," explains his executioner. The
truth, or efforts to communicate what one believes to be
the truth, must be suppressed at all costs, if a system of
oppression is to be maintained.

Ellison's novel, *Invisible Man*, has many points in
common with *The Man Who Lived Underground*, not
so much in style as in content. The most obvious simi-
larity is the device of an underground existence, literal
as well as symbolic hibernation. The prologue and epilogue of *Invisible Man* show the protagonist in a warm
hole in the ground, the basement of a New York City
building, which he has wired and lighted with 1,369
electric bulbs. Here he rethinks the nature of his life,
trying to define himself and his universe. He has the
feeling that much of his life has been a dream, a nightmare. In the epilogue there is an allusion to Conrad's
Heart of Darkness as a journey into the inner recesses of
the mind. (Ellison's novel makes many allusions to other
writers and their work; Wright's novelette does not,
although its very last line, "lost in the heart of the
earth," may be an allusion to Conrad's short novel.)

Like Wright's story, Ellison's makes a point of
obscuring the protagonist's name. Wright's character
gives his name once, midway through the story, and then
forgets it himself; Ellison's character never is named.

The novel proper, sandwiched between the prologue and epilogue, is a flashback to the life Ellison's
main character is trying to sort out. In a paint factory
(chapter 10), the protagonist, seeking a job, is sent

deep into the earth, to the furnace room. Here he meets
Brockway, a black furnace stoker who, like the furnace
stoker in *The Man Who Lived Underground*, has adjusted to a dark, underground world. In fact, he feels so
powerful that he has the sense of controlling the building by means of his furnace valves.

In *Invisible Man* the truth of existence is not, as in
Wright's story, suppressed by gunning down a protagonist eager to communicate it to the police. It is suppressed in the novel proper by a "jive" game—or "con"
game—that the protagonist and another character, Tod
Clifton, are put through. As Ellison describes it, it is a
sort of "Keep This Nigger-Boy Running" game played
by con artists in education, represented by Bledsoe, an
Uncle Tom president of a southern black college;
Norton, a white philanthropist not unlike Dalton in
Native Son; Rinehart, a black preacher hustling and
fooling the people; Ras the Exhorter, a Marcus Garvey-
type black nationalist portrayed as an irrational ex-
tremist; Brother Jack, an unscrupulous member of the
"Brotherhood," *i.e.*, the Communist Party. While the
game of fooling the protagonist and Tod Clifton (a
promising young black man like the protagonist) is run,
the furnace tender plays at subverting the white establishment.

By 1944 Wright felt that the American Communist
Party was almost as intolerably oppressive as American
capitalism. The Communist hierarchy had often found
ideological "faults" in his thinking. When they criticized
Native Son, reversed their position from opposition to
entering World War II to active participation, and
shifted their emphasis from amelioration of economic
conditions and civil rights to the war effort, he had to
assert his disagreement in the only way possible. Wright
left the Party in 1944. The irreconcilable conflict was

between individual conscience and the Party's authoritarian demands upon the intellectuals in its ranks. As Wright said in "I Tried To Be a Communist," a widely publicized essay, "I wanted to be a Communist, but my kind of Communist."[30]

Although Wright had too much character to be the unquestioning servant of any group, he felt his break with the Communist Party as a heavy blow; it did not so much remove a weight as add another, greater one. He felt more keenly the isolation of a man who has lived underground, the compulsion to discover and reveal to someone some small measure of truth that would make the darkness of his cave less dark. "I headed toward home alone, really alone now," without the support of the Party. "Perhaps, I thought, out of my tortured feelings I could fling a spark into this darkness. I would try, not because I wanted to, but because I felt that I had to if I were to live at all."[31]

Regrets at having been used by the Communist Party? No. The Party had taught Wright much and given him a sense of hope when he had needed it most. "I remembered the stories I had written, the stories in which I had assigned a role of honor and glory to the Communist Party, and I was glad that they were down in black and white, were finished. For I knew in my heart that I should never be able to feel with that simple sharpness about life, should never again express such passionate hope, should never again make so total a commitment of faith."[32]

Wright's thoughts turned back to the lonely days of his childhood and in *Black Boy: A Record of Childhood and Youth* (1945) he poetically presented, and interpreted from an adult perspective, the excitement and imagination of youth yearning for identity and meaning.

Each event spoke with a cryptic tongue. And the moments of living slowly revealed their coded meanings. There was the wonder I felt when I first saw a brace of mountainlike, spotted, black-and-white horses clopping down a dusty road through clouds of powdered clay.

There was the delight I caught in seeing long straight rows of red and green vegetables stretching away in the sun to the bright horizon.

There was the faint, cool kiss of sensuality when dew came on to my cheeks and shins as I ran down the wet green garden paths in the early morning.

There was the vague sense of the infinite as I looked down upon the yellow, dreaming waters of the Mississippi River from the verdant bluffs of Natchez.

There were the echoes of nostalgia I heard in the crying strings of wild geese winging south against a bleak, autumn sky.

. . . .

There was the yearning for identification loosed in me by the sight of a solitary ant carrying a burden upon a mysterious journey.

Blended with these gentle images are images of childhood fascination with death:

There was the disdain that filled me as I tortured a delicate, blue-pink crawfish that huddled fearfully in the mudsill of a rusty tin can.

. . . .

There was the experience of feeling death without dying that came from watching a chicken leap about blindly after its neck had been snapped by a quick twist of my father's wrist.

And there are youthful superstitions:

Up or down the wet or dusty streets, indoors or out, the days and nights began to spell out magic possibilities.

If I pulled a hair from a horse's tail and sealed it in a jar of my own urine, the hair would turn overnight into a snake.

If I passed a Catholic sister or mother dressed in black and smiled and allowed her to see my teeth, I would surely die.

If I walked under a leaning ladder, I would certainly have bad luck.

If I kissed my elbow, I would turn into a girl.

. . . .

If the stars twinkled more than usual on any given night, it meant that the angels in heaven were happy and were flitting across the floors of heaven: and since stars were merely holes ventilating heaven, the twinkling came from the angels flitting past the holes that admitted air into the holy home of God.

. . . .

Anything seemed possible, likely, feasible, because I wanted everything to be possible . . . Because I had no power to make things happen outside of me in the objective world, I made things happen within.[33]

Black Boy, certainly among Wright's most moving works, recaptures, as few autobiographies of youth can, the pain and fear, pleasures and hopes, innocence and growth, the metamorphosis toward an uncertain adulthood. *Black Boy* is *Native Son* without the thin veneer of fiction. Like so much of Wright's fiction, it focuses on children curious about life yet vulnerable to the sociological and psychological oppression that forces them to grow up early.

In 1945 Wright's continuing interest in sociology led him to write an introduction for an extensive, two-volume study of urban Negro life in Chicago, *Black Metropolis*, by St. Clair Drake and Horace R. Cayton. In it he predicted that fascistic methods and violence

would come to Chicago and the rest of America if conditions were not radically improved.

If, in reading my novel, *Native Son,* you doubted the
reality of Bigger Thomas, then examine the delinquency
rates cited in this book; if, in reading my autobiography,
Black Boy, you doubted the picture of family life shown
there, then study the figures on family disorganization given
here. *Black Metropolis* describes the processes that mold
Negro life as we know it today, processes that make the
majority of Negroes on Chicago's South Side sixth-graders,
processes that make 65 per cent of all Negroes on Chicago's
South Side earn their living by manual labor. After study-
ing the social processes in this book, you cannot expect
Negro life to be other than what it is. . . .

Do not hold a light attitude toward the slums of Chicago's South Side. Remember that Hitler came out of such
a slum. Remember that Chicago could be the Vienna of
American Fascism! . . .

Can America change these conditions? Or is it hopeless to expect an understanding of this problem? If this
problem cannot be mastered, then one thing is fairly cer-
tain: The liberals, the intellectuals, the artists, the students,
Communists, Socialists, New Dealers, all who hope for life
and peace will lose to war. In short, what happened in
Europe during the past twenty years will happen here.

I'm not naive enough to believe that many will heed
such Cassandra-like warnings, for not many people really
believe that any such crisis exists. . . .[34]

This warning, dire and pessimistic, came more than
twenty years before the rioting in the late 1960's. It
long preceded James Baldwin's warning in *The Fire
Next Time* (1963).

A year later, the periodical *Twice a Year* published a sociological essay by Wright, "Urban Misery in
an American City."[35] Here Wright uses specific case
studies to show how social conditions in New York's

Harlem have affected black family life and produced juvenile delinquency. He also quotes from Gunnar Myrdal's important sociological study, *An American Dilemma*, first published in 1944.

The years 1946 and 1947 were critical in Richard Wright's life. His decision to leave the Communist Party was equalled by a similarly difficult decision to leave his country for France. Like the mature James Joyce, the mature Wright came to realize that he could not broaden his artistic and personal freedom without leaving the oppressive soil from which he had sprung. In order to make effective use of his roots he had to supplement psychic distance with physical distance. Joyce left his home, his religion, and his country, "[t]o discover the mode of life or of art whereby your spirit could express itself in unfettered freedom. . . . I will not serve that in which I no longer believe, whether it call itself my home, my fatherland, or my church."[36] Wright had to leave home for the alien North, and later, for the East that was Europe. He had already left Christianity and Communism.

Wright saw that Chicago and New York were no better than Mississippi as places where a black man and his white wife could raise children, where a black man would be treated as a man. After his 1939 marriage to Dhima Rose Meadman had broken up, he had married, in 1941, another white girl, Ellen Poplar, a Brooklyn girl he had met at a Communist Party function before his first marriage. Wright now had to consider a wife's happiness and a daughter's future (Julia, born in 1942); he also had his own creative and personal spirit to protect. Neither in Brooklyn nor in Greenwich Village would he and his family be free from searing prejudice.

In May 1946 the Wrights went to Paris; however, the following January they returned to the United States.

Wright had liked the intellectual environment of Paris, but he was still not convinced that he could do better work there than in New York. A few months back in New York changed his mind. He again found the racial atmosphere intolerable, and he felt that he would go mad if he remained in America. Packing all his books, jazz recordings, and other belongings, he returned to Paris in August 1947. Except for a brief stay in London, Paris was to be his home for the rest of his life.

3

Paris
(1947-1952)

When World War II ended in 1945, many black soldiers who had experienced an absence of color prejudice for the first time decided to remain abroad rather than return home. They were soon joined by black writers and artists who could scrape up the fare for the trip, and who like Richard Wright sought freedom from insanity and needed a climate that would encourage their creative development. Among these black expatriates were novelists James Baldwin, Chester Himes, and William Gardner Smith, artists Ollie Harrington, Larry Potter, and Herb Gentry, actor Gordon Heath, jazz musician Art Simmons, and symphonic orchestra conductor Dean Dixon.

A favorite meeting place was the small Café Tournon, on the left bank's rue de Tournon, facing the French Senate building and the Luxembourg Gardens. Only a short distance from Wright's apartment at 14 rue Monsieur le Prince, they sat and talked at the sidewalk tables or stood around the American pinball machine which Wright loved to play. Often they gathered at a restaurant near Montmartre run by Leroy Haynes, a black southerner and ex-G.I., at 3 rue Clauzel, just off the Place St. Georges. Here they ate southern fried chicken, chitterlings, pig feet, black-eyed peas, red beans, and the closest thing to collard greens chef Leroy could find in Paris.

For the most part they stayed together, easily dating French women but not mixing well with the many black Africans in the city. Their cultures were too different.

Wright and other American blacks at first felt that Paris was relatively free from racial discrimination. Gradually, however, they realized that Frenchmen saw them as curiosities, less tribal than the African blacks, to which they were inevitably compared. In the late

1950's Wright felt that the virus of racism was openly spreading in France. Since his daughter Julia was then attending Cambridge, in 1959 Wright obtained a three-month visa and spent that fall in London. During this time he applied for a permanent visa, but pressure was mounting to limit nonwhite immigration to England, and the request was denied.

During his first years in Paris Richard Wright wrote comparatively little. In the period between 1947 and 1953 no new books appeared. He was enjoying the novelty of racial freedom in France but still feeling the strong effects of leaving the Party, the loneliness of having to make his own way without support.

Wright was now faced with the necessity of read-justing his writing habits to a new environment, and at the same time he was bothered by a persistent feeling that he should change the direction of his writing. These feelings of dislocation and change interfered with his work, as he told his long-time editor, Edward Aswell, in a letter dated August 21, 1955.

One of the first people to try to make Richard Wright feel at home in Paris was Gertrude Stein. He had always admired her work, and during his first trip to Paris, shortly before her death (July 27, 1946), he visited her apartment for long talks.

Others who befriended Wright during this period included Jean-Paul Sartre and Simone de Beauvoir, both of whom he had met earlier in the United States. For several years he was friendly but not intimate with African writers he met through *Présence Africaine*, an African journal started in Paris in 1947. Its founder, Alioune Diop, a Sengalese intellectual, introduced Wright to some of the best writers from Africa and the West Indies. Among these men were Aimé Césaire (Martinique), Léon Damas (French Guiana), and

Léopold Sédar Senghor (Senegal).

Wright did a few short pieces for *Présence Afri-caine* and served on the journal's board of patrons to-gether with Sartre, Albert Camus, and André Gide. When in the 1950's *Présence Africaine* organized the Society of African Culture to encourage the spread of black culture, Wright lent a hand.

In 1950 he was a central force in the formation of an organization for blacks, the Franco-American Fellow-ship. Within this fellowship Wright sought to gather the many black American expatriates "to promote social and cultural relations; and to heighten the consciousness of its members in relation to the urgent issues confront-ing the world today."[1] This organization was unsuccess-ful because its leading members pulled in opposite directions and could not agree upon goals.

During the period 1947-1952, Wright was quite busy with a movie script for *Native Son*, the writing of a few short stories and articles on the racial problem in the United States, and mostly unrewarding efforts to write on subjects other than racism.

Work on the *Native Son* movie during the years 1949 and 1950 (the film was released in 1951) was certainly a major factor in keeping Wright from continu-ing his efforts as a novelist. He not only did the script but also occupied himself with business arrangements for producing and distributing the film. In addition, having decided to play the role of Bigger Thomas him-self, he had the difficult task of learning his lines and taking off enough weight to look a bit more like a twenty-year-old slum kid.

Wright had previously worked on other scripts. He had collaborated with Paul Green on a stage version of *Native Son*, produced by Orson Welles's Mercury Theatre. With Canada Lee in the role of Bigger Thomas the play had been a success on Broadway, premiering at the St. James Theatre, March 24, 1941. Several unsuccessful film projects never reached production. One of these was *Melody Unlimited,* the story of the famous Jubilee Singers, a group from Fisk University that toured the United States and England in the 1870's to raise money for the building of Negro schools in the South. It was written in 1944. Some time later Wright collaborated with novelist George Crosby on a filmscript entitled *The Last Flight* (Columbia Pictures). The story dealt with an American fascist who works for the Nazis as a broadcaster until Germany begins to collapse, and who then returns to the United States. The film was never made.[2]

Nor were producers any more receptive to his *Native Son* filmscript. No Hollywood studio was willing to make the movie without watering down its strongly critical view of American racial conditions. One Hollywood producer proposed making the character of Bigger a white man. Eventually Wright decided to have the film shot in Argentina, which as he saw it was not overly dependent upon United States foreign aid.[3]

On their way to Argentina, Wright and the film's French director, Pierre Chenal, stopped in Chicago to film a few exterior shots. This return to Chicago after so many years stirred bitter memories for Wright and he wrote an article for *Ebony,* "The Shame of Chicago."[4]

When the filming of *Native Son* was completed it underwent drastic cutting, against Wright's wishes. Next came a variety of distribution difficulties.[5] From all appearances the film was artistically and financially unsuccessful.

During these years, despite Wright's growing desire to write on other subjects, all of the relatively few arti-

cles and stories he was able to publish dealt with racism.
He published English articles in *Présence Africaine*, and
with his French improving, French-language articles
in *France Observateur, Preuves, Les Temps Modernes,
Franc Tireur*, and a few other French publications. Some
of his material also appeared in *Encounter* (England),
and *Ebony*. The only fiction to be published in these
years was one short story, "The Man Who Killed a
Shadow." In 1946 it was published in a French translation, and it was not until three years later that *Zero*, a
magazine issued in Paris by American expatriates, published the original English text.[6]

"The Man Who Killed a Shadow" recalls some of
the thematic elements of *Native Son*, and it demonstrates
Wright's continuing interest in the psychology of fear.
The central character, Saul, is a young black man afraid
of the shadows of his fears and suffering from an inferi-
ority complex. He had previously been employed as an
exterminator of rats, a job he enjoyed because the dead
rats were concrete evidence that his work produced
results. Now a janitor in the National Cathedral in
Washington, D.C., Saul is teased by a sexually appealing
white woman. When he ignores her, she calls him "black
nigger," and he slaps her. She screams. The same fear
that had led Bigger Thomas to kill Mary Dalton now
drives Saul to murder. He aims a blow at her head with
his powerful arm, and he cracks her skull. To stop her
screams he hits her again, chokes her, and finally stabs
her. He mops up the dead woman's blood with her own
pink panties, not pausing to look at her uncovered groin.
Later, awakening at home from a sound sleep, he has a
dream-like awareness of what he has done, "as though
he were looking . . . at a scene being flashed upon the
screen of a movie house." This use of movies as an ex-

pression of the blur between dreams and reality is a device that Wright had previously employed in *Native Son* and *The Man Who Lived Underground*. The short story ends with a brief but not climactic scene at Saul's courtroom trial, again somewhat paralleling the development of *Native Son*.

Three short stories written sometime in the 1950's, but not published until the late 1950's,[7] have in common a sense of humor rarely seen in the author's other works.

The setting for "Man, God Ain't Like That . . ." includes the jungles of Africa and Paris. The main character is Babu, a stereotyped savage straight from a Tarzan comic strip or movie. When Babu is hit by a white man's car, instead of becoming angry, he apologizes for denting the fender. The white man, an American painter living in Paris, takes him back to France as a curiosity, and employs him as a servant. Babu thinks the white man, John, whom he calls Massa, is Christ. Pictures in missionary school books he had seen showed God as white. He assumes that Massa is a missionary God come to lift up the black people as He had lifted up the whites. (Missionaries had partially "civilized" Babu, teaching him to sing Methodist hymns, but he still carries a suitcase filled with bones of his dead father and meant for use in tribal rituals.) Babu kills John in order to witness a holy resurrection, another rebirth of Christ. He reasons that one ritual murder of Christ resulted in the building of a magnificent white civilization, and that maybe a second ritual murder of Christ would result in the building of a great black civilization. Wright satirizes both the white man's colonial mentality and the African natives caught between ancient tribal beliefs and the teachings of white European Christianity. The idea for

Wright's story is excellent but the characters and the narrative are undeveloped and contrived. Yet on the level of fantasy-satire, the story is funny.

In "Man of All Work" an unemployed black man disguises himself as a woman in order to get a maid's job. He is almost raped by the white head of the house, who finds him attractive. The black man reveals himself and extorts money from the surprised lecher. Like "Man, God Ain't Like That . . . ," this story sardonically mocks white racial attitudes. Both stories work entirely through dialogue, and they were first written as radio scripts for transmission in Germany. "Man of All Work" is only mildly amusing, but "Man, God Ain't Like That . . ." is a prime example of a black-style, tongue-in-cheek tall tale.

The third story, "Big Black Good Man," laughs at the unjustified fears a large and very black man arouses in some white people. In a sleazy waterfront hotel in Copenhagen a night clerk is frightened half to death by a massive giant of a man, an American Negro, asking for room, bottle, and broad. Later the black man returns to the hotel desk, silently seizes the trembling old man by the throat, and then calmly releases him. After spending six nights with whiskey and a whore, he makes the clerk a present of six new shirts. Amused by his obvious fear of blacks, the Negro had seized the clerk's throat only to measure his neck size. The story, though somewhat amusing, is another tall tale—and a labored one at that.

4

Paris
(1953-1957)

The Outsider, published in 1953, was Wright's first new book since *Black Boy* (1945), and his first novel since *Native Son* (1940). Although the American press had largely ignored the recently released film version of *Native Son*, it did not ignore *The Outsider*. It was reviewed almost as widely as *Native Son* had been thirteen years before. The American reading public may have forgotten Wright, but the critics were curious to see what had happened to the native son. Had exile hurt his work? The reviews were mixed but mostly negative. Wright, they said, had lost much of his power, and his roots were gone, no more than a memory. The same conclusions would later be reached about *The Long Dream* and *Eight Men*.

Much could be made of the negative influence of European exile. The first novel to be written in Europe bears the dedication, "For Rachel, my daughter who was born on alien soil," and the last collection of fiction to be prepared for publication just before his death, *Eight Men*, bears the dedication, "To my friends, Hélène, Michel, Thierry, Maurice-Bokanowski, whose kindness has made me feel at home in an alien land." In the dedications prefacing *The Outsider* and *Eight Men*, one could emphasize either Wright's sense of being "in an alien land," or, in the *Eight Men* dedication, his feeling of being "at home."

The truth of the matter may be that the strengths or weaknesses of the fiction and nonfiction written in Europe are not attributable to any physical or mental displacement, but to the continuation of Wright's literary experimentation with methods of expressing his sociological and psychological explorations.

In *Native Son* Wright had gradually abandoned the narrative device—a psychological case study of a black man, with a measure of esthetic distance—for a more

64

frontal attack: a propagandistic essay in the style of
work he had done for the *New Masses* and *Left Front*.
The last third of *Native Son* is such a polemic. In *The
Man Who Lived Underground* Wright had written a
more unified story, free of polemic digressions.

While *Underground* is a strong, unflawed work,
both *Native Son* and *The Outsider* falter in places, with
The Outsider being by far the weaker of the two. It contains fewer of *Native Son*'s strengths and most of its
weaknesses. Where *Native Son* is powerful and believ-
able, *The Outsider* borders upon the melodramatic.
Where *Native Son* has narrative muscle and raw, yet
eloquent dialogue, *The Outsider* sounds unconvincingly
intellectual. While *Native Son* avoids polemic until the
last third, the courtroom scene in particular, such inter-
ruptions are plentiful in *The Outsider*.

Cross Damon, the outsider, is an intellectual version of Bigger Thomas. He is experiencing an identity
crisis brought on by a hostile white world, a loving
white girl, and conflict with the Communist Party. His
reaction to these nightmarish problems is even more violent than that of Bigger Thomas. He is responsible for
four murders and one suicide. Like Bigger, he is already
a vicious, angry man before the novel begins, and he is
already on the brink of self-destruction. He can reach
out to a man who is not black, but only if that man (Ely
Houston, the hunchbacked district attorney from New
York) is like himself crippled, outside all groups, isolated. Like Wright, Cross had striven to be seen as an
individual, apart from race. Like Meursault, the existen-
tialist protagonist in Camus's *L'Etranger* (which could
be translated as *The Outsider* instead of *The Stranger*),
Cross's life mixes with death in an inseparable blend,
one indistinguishable from the other, both without
meaning.

At one point in the novel, Cross witnesses "his own" funeral[1] and his sense of the unreal quality of his life increases. He had earlier listened to a radio announcement on the wreck of a Chicago elevated train, and heard his own name mistakenly reported as the 44th victim. He can now look at his life in a detached dream-like way, his "reality" coming to him from a radio box, or a newspaper, in much the same manner as it comes to the protagonists in *Native Son* and *The Man Who Lived Underground*.

Like Jake Jackson in *Lawd Today*, and like Wright himself, Cross has worked at a mentally deadening job, "sorting mail like a sleepwalker." Now he has the intriguing possibility of beginning life all over again. But he cannot improve the course of his life. With a new name (Lionel Lane), taken from a freshly dug grave in a New York cemetery, he plunges ahead into murder and violence; the same problem of self-identity plagues him.

Early in Wright's novel Cross is asked by friends why he reads so many books. His answer is that he is looking for something but he doesn't know what, and that he has not found it. He has the feeling that these friends are really outside his life. His real problem is his relationship to himself: he had married and dropped out of college, become "choked with self-hate" and so filled with despair that he contemplated suicide.

Cross's relationship with his mother contains a love-hate vacillation. He associates her with the God in which she so firmly and so simply believes. He would reject that God as a force of hate and punishment rather than of love, but this would also mean rejecting his mother. His love-hate feelings are a symbolic cross he must bear, an ambiguous problem he can neither understand nor resolve. And he is afraid. "Afraid of what?

Nothing exactly, precisely . . . And this constituted his sense of dread."[2]

Wright asks why many people are fated to be like the Bible's Job, sharing the same ambiguity of existence, "fated to live a never-ending debate between themselves and their sense of what they believed life should be [.] . . . [I]t was as though one was angry but did not know toward what or whom the anger should be directed; it was as though one felt betrayed, but could never determine the manner of the betrayal."[3] In an epigraph to the novel Wright quotes from the poetry of William Blake, whose mystical symbolism attracted him, and from the Book of Job. God advises Job to obey His word without questioning the suffering of the righteous, "Mark me, and be astonished/ And lay your hand upon your mouth." Cross, like Wright himself, sees religion as a refuge from thinking, a refuge sought by the oppressed, even though it is only an illusion. "How lucky they were, those black worshipers, to be able to feel lonely together."[4] Cross partly envies his mother her religious belief, her refuge, although his intelligence prevents him from using religion as an opiate. "To think I named you Cross after the Cross of Jesus," wails his desperately Christian mother.[5]

After the train wreck that buried his old identity, after witnessing "his own" funeral, and after killing his friend Joe for recognizing him in a cheap hotel, Cross takes a train from Chicago to New York. On this train he meets a Catholic priest, and through him, the hunchback attorney Ely Houston. As he looks at the priest, Cross thinks of Freud's writing on totems and taboos, and he visualizes the priest as a dressed-up savage. Cross sees that without God he must bear complete responsibility for his own actions, and that his standards of criticism are more exacting than those of God. He also

confronts the knowledge that cut off from the promise
of religion he has only this one life, a life that may contain and mean nothing. " 'Maybe man is nothing in particular,' Cross said gropingly. 'Maybe that's the terror
of it.' "6

Later in the novel, this uncertainty hardens, becoming a negation of life and the thought processes. "Cross
had had no party, no myths, no tradition, no race, no
soil, no culture, and no ideas—except perhaps the idea
that ideas in themselves were, at best, dubious!"7

Under the assumed name of Lionel Lane, Cross
Damon begins working for the Communist Party in
New York, but he only uses the Party as a cover and has
no sense of commitment to it. Wright's very harsh, very
negative portrayals of Communist members make it
clear that he now considered the Party to be merely an
exploiter of men's dreams and desires. One of the novel's
minor characters is Bob Hunter, a Negro who, after being fired from his job as a dining-car waiter, is recruited
by the Party, used for its ends, and then discarded. Bad
faith, according to Cross Damon and Richard Wright,
is present everywhere. But people fool themselves even
more than they are fooled by others: they fool themselves into believing that their dreams and desires are
attainable. "Cross was convinced that bad faith of some
degree was an indigenous part of living. The daily stifling
of one's sense of terror in the face of life, the far-flung
conspiracy of pretending that life was tending toward a
goal of redemption, the reasonless assumption that one's
dreams and desires were realizable—all of these hourly,
human feelings were bad faith."8

In a scene of grotesque violence, Cross beats to
death both a Communist Party official (Gilbert Blount)
and a fascistic landlord ("Herr" Langley Herndon),
calling them both insects. He then attempts to burn an

incriminating bloody handkerchief in an incinerator. (The scene is reminiscent of Bigger Thomas's incineration of evidence in *Native Son.*) Unknown to Cross, the handkerchief is not destroyed. Later it is recovered by Jack Hilton, a Communist Party organizer, who uses it in an attempt to insure Cross's loyalty to the Party.

Cross eventually kills Hilton too. He does so not just from fear of having his earlier crimes revealed to the police, but because of a growing conviction that the Communist officials he has known are as bad as fascists —insects treating other men as insects. Cross recognizes that he himself has been sufficiently brutalized to brutalize other men.

As he returns to his apartment, in the building owned by the murdered Langley Herndon, Cross is picked up by the police for questioning. District Attorney Houston quizzes him and assesses the evidence. Though he lets Cross go free, he says, in effect, I do not have sufficient evidence to convict you in court, so you're free—but not really free. You made your own law, now live by it. Eat and sleep with the memory of what you did. This psychology of toying with a suspect's mind is very much like the central action in Dostoyevsky's *Crime and Punishment.*

Soon after, as he walks along the street Cross hears "water gurgling in the gutters, running toward the conduits of the sewers." (This short scene brings to mind the underground world that had been both a haven and a death trap in *The Man Who Lived Underground.*) Cross enters a movie theater and sees "shadows on the screen without understanding their import." On emerging from the theater, he realizes that he is being followed by two Party agents. He goes into a second movie house, "into the sheltering darkness." In a sense this movie house, like all others, is a make-believe house, not a place of real protection and warmth. Leaving the theater three hours later, he is shot and fatally wounded. He dies in the hospital with District Attorney Houston at his side.

Although Cross's predominant attitude is that life is meaningless, twice he has the feeling that he can help other people to avoid the road he has taken and to find definition for their own lives. One of these moments occurs when he begins to love a white woman, Eva Blount, the Communist official's wife. Despite evidence that she loves him *because* he is black, he wants to help her. " 'Eva, I'd feel happier than I ever dreamed if I could make you believe in life again. . . .'[9] 'You *can*! You must.' . . . Could he allow her to love him for his color when being a Negro was the least important thing in his life?"[10] At the moment of his death, Cross confides to the district attorney, whom he has almost accepted as a friend, "I wish I had some way to give the meaning of my life to others. . . . To make a bridge from man to man."[11]

From the standpoint of its prose style, *The Outsider* is weak. Too often there are awkward and inappropriate juxtapositions of slang with overly formal diction. For example, one passage reads, "The assumptive promises he had welshed on were not materially anchored, yet they were indubitably the things of this world, the axis of daily existence." And once Cross is described as in bed "beseeching sleep," and later that same night he realizes that "his search for surcease was hopeless."

Too often the narrative flow is interrupted or replaced by long, essay-like polemics. These lectures resemble the long speeches of Mr. Max in the final third of *Native Son*. The lectures, delivered at frequent intervals by Mr. Houston, Mr. Max's counterpart, and occassionally by the intellectual Cross Damon himself, cover the fields of sociology and psychology.

Ely Houston psychoanalyzes Cross Damon, and Cross Damon psychoanalyzes Ely Houston in dissertations that completely arrest the narrative's flow. " 'Some men are so placed in life by accident of race or birth that what they see is terrifying,' Houston said, carried away by his theme."[12] As Cross listens to Houston's psychological analysis of an outsider, he psychoanalyzes Houston, seeing that "Houston was caught in the same psychological trap. . . . Houston was an impulsive criminal who protected himself by hunting down other criminals! How cleverly the man had worked out his life, had balanced his emotional drives!"[13]

At another point in the novel Cross gives a fifteen-page lecture on modern industrialization and its effect upon human life.[14] It's not unlike an essay included in Wright's *White Man, Listen!* (1957) and entitled "Tradition and Industrialization."

The Outsider ends with a moral, delivered, ostensibly, by the dying Cross. Wright is again lecturing, as he had done in *Native Son*, afraid that the narrative may not speak strongly enough for itself. "Men hate themselves and it makes them hate others. . . . We're strangers to ourselves. . . . Don't think I'm so odd and strange. . . .[15] I'm not. . . .[16] I'm legion. . . . For a long time he [man] has been sleeping, wrapped in a dream. . . .[17] He is awakening now, awakening from his dream and finding himself in a waking nightmare. . . ."[18]

Just before dying, Cross proclaims his essential innocence to Houston. When he is asked how his life had been, Cross replies that it was horrible, all of it. Why horrible? "Because in my heart . . . I'm . . . I felt . . . I'm *innocent*. . . . That's what made the horror. . . ."[19] "Shadows" descend upon him and he is dead.

In *The Man Who Lived Underground* Fred Daniels had said that he was guilty and that all the people he could see from his hidden world were guilty. They were guilty because they felt guilty. In *The Outsider* Cross Damon declares that he is innocent. Why? Because he was forced to lead a life of constant punishment, punishment inflicted *before* his crimes.

Savage Holiday was published a year after *The Outsider*, with much difficulty. It had been turned down by Harper, and Wright's agent, Paul Reynolds, agreed that the novel was inferior and would add nothing positive to Wright's reputation.[20] The novel was not submitted to any other major publisher but was released as a paperback original by Avon Books (1954). The second of Wright's books to appear under the aegis of a firm other than Harper's—*12 Million Black Voices* was published by Viking Press—it was not reviewed by the American press. A year later the French translation appeared and was favorably reviewed by French critics.

Savage Holiday is Wright's only published effort to write a psychological study that studiously avoids the racial problem. Its central character is Erskine Fowler, a white man who has just completed thirty years with a New York insurance firm. Even though he is still only forty-three, he is forced to retire. At a testimonial dinner in his honor, he is given an inscribed gold medal in recognition of his rise from errand boy to company executive. He is forced to take part in "the game of make-believe," to laugh and seem generally pleased with the speaker's words of praise and the prospects for retirement. Scarcely half an hour before the banquet he had fought with company executives over the retirement, but they were convinced his ideas were behind the times.

One Sunday soon after, Erskine finds himself locked out of his apartment, naked. (The door had slammed shut as he attempted to retrieve his scattered Sunday newspaper.) Trying to get back in, he scales an outside balcony, frightening a little boy into falling to his death. Erskine begins to assess the extent of his own guilt and the role of the boy's somewhat fast and loose mother. We learn that Tony, the boy, was afraid of naked men because Mabel, his mother, left her bedroom door open when having intercourse with men, and Tony thought the naked men were attacking his mother.

The woman, ostensibly an opposite to his own character, attracts Erskine. He hates and loves her. He wants to marry Mabel, or, failing that, be around her enough to psychoanalyze her. Because she refuses to devote time to him, he knifes her to death, violently stabbing her again and again until his arm is tired. In the moments that follow, his thoughts flash back to his childhood and a doll he had "killed." He had, he remembers, made believe that the doll was his own mother, whom all the boys he knew had said was a bad woman.

As the adult Erskine hastens to confess his murder of Mabel, toying, as he often did, with pencils in his pocket, he recalls the colored pencils with which the child Erskine had colored a picture of the murdered doll.

Following Wright's custom in some of his other books, epigraphs from literature, philosophy, psychology, and other fields precede each major division of the novel. Here he quotes from—among other works— Sandor Ferenczi's *Sunday Neuroses*, Freud's *Totem and*

Taboo, and Theodore Reik's *The Unknown Murderer*. The extract from Freud reads, ". . . in the very nature of a holiday there is excess; the holiday mood is brought about by the release of what is forbidden."

The novel does not succeed; its story is too labored, an abstractly conceived patchwork of Freudian symbols and dreams.

The rejection of *Savage Holiday* by Harper rankled and worried Wright. He wrote to his old editor, Edward Aswell, August 21, 1955, that he was unsure about how readers would react to future novels that dealt with subjects other than race. Anticipating difficulty in gaining acceptance by a public that associated his name with racial themes, Wright had considered publishing *Savage Holiday* under an assumed name. However, he assured Aswell that his desire to write more novels on broader subjects was not shaken and that he was planning a novel to be titled *A Strange Daughter*, the story of an American white girl troubled by a sexual problem which the letter does not detail.

This same unpublished letter goes on to project a series of novels, including a story about the Aztec king Montezuma. (Wright had perhaps gotten this idea from his 1940 trip to Mexico with his first wife, Dhima.) Despite its negative reception, he intended to include *Savage Holiday* in this series. The common denominator in these seemingly disparate works would be individual studies of how society can break men, men of many nationalities, religions, and races. The projected series was to be called *Celebration*—the problem to be sung or posed in many ways.

Looking back at Harper's rejection of *Savage Holiday*, Wright would conclude that the publishers, as well as Edward Aswell, his favorite editor, and Paul R. Reynolds, his literary agent, were interested in seeing him continue what had long been a successful vein, not moving in new directions. Wright may have seen that they were correct; nevertheless, there remained a residue of resentment that he could not write and publish anything he wanted to.

In 1953, the same year that *The Outsider* was being published in New York, and a few months after completing the first draft of *Savage Holiday*, Wright took a trip to Ghana, in West Africa. The result, *Black Power: A Record of Reactions in a Land of Pathos* (New York, 1954), is the attempt of an American black man to understand the social, economic and political structure of a foreign country about which he and other Americans knew little. However, Wright's investigations were to antagonize blacks both in Africa and in Paris. They were resentful and their pride was hurt. Wright, they felt, was not a black brother but just another unenlightened foreign meddler.

Although Wright had disclaimed any intention of producing a scholarly, authoritative study of Ghana, his book was invariably read not as a personal "record of reactions" but as a claim to expertise about the land. In any case, in preparation for this trip Wright did read about the country, its past, present and projected future.

In the first chapter of *Black Power* Wright speaks of his fears in going to Africa. He tries to anticipate and analyze his reactions to a land where blacks are in the majority, reactions to a land that should be home to him, reactions to a land that sold his ancestors into slavery.

Wright antagonized many Africans with his descriptions of the primitive and undeveloped aspects of Ghanian social, political, and economic life. He felt that the most important obstacle Ghana and the rest of black Africa had to overcome in their struggle to be free of

outside control was the tribal structure of African society, which inhibited modern development. He con-
cluded that Africa could not overcome this obstacle
unless the lives of its people were subjected to a form of
militarization that would give "form, organization, direction, meaning, and a sense of justification to those
lives. . . . I'm speaking of a temporary discipline
that will unite the nation, sweep out the tribal cobwebs,
and place the feet of the masses upon a basis of reality."[21] He spoke of nothing less than the complete
change of social structure, and this mammoth job cannot be accomplished with "the continued existence of
those parasitic chiefs who have too long bled and mis-
led a naive people."[22]

To a large extent, *Black Power*, like *12 Million
Black Voices*, is a Marxist analysis of black economy,
history, and living conditions. Marxism played an important, positive role in the development of an independent Africa, providing the guiding principles for leaders
like Ghana's Kwame Nkrumah. Another African leader,
Léopold Sédar Senghor, the poet-president of Senegal,
wrote that "Marxism was to be our first instrument of
liberation."[23]

Both the trip (1953) and the book (1954) were
largely inspired by an important friendship Wright de-
veloped with George Padmore. In London, 1947,
Wright had met this man who was to become a major
influence upon his thought.

A West Indian, Padmore was born Malcolm Nurse
in Trinidad, 1902 or 1903—the date is uncertain. Educated in United States universities, Nurse joined the
Communist Party in New York in the late 1920's and
changed his name to George Padmore. He felt that the
Communist movement could work for the elimination of
all forms of racial oppression, including colonialism and

neo-colonialism. After traveling on Party business all over Europe, he had a falling out with the Party and left the movement in 1934. London became his permanent residence in 1935 and here he devoted his time to working for African independence, seeking some method of uniting black men politically and economically. He envisioned the day when Africa would expel western imperialists and stand up as a united power, a United States of Africa.

In 1957 George Padmore left London for Ghana, where he became an advisor to Kwame Nkrumah, the leader of the newly independent state formed that same year from the British colony, the Gold Coast. With Nkrumah, Padmore worked to transform Ghana from a conglomerate of tribal loyalties into a united country that would hopefully become the nucleus of a vast, strong Pan-African nation. Death in 1959 ended Padmore's role in leading the African revolution, and the overthrow of the allegedly corrupt Nkrumah, by an army coup in 1966, ended what Pan-Africanists considered a noble effort, but what the United States government characterized as a Communist conspiracy. Nkrumah died in 1972, an exile in neighboring Guinea.

Nkrumah, in his book *Africa Must Unite* (1963), speaks of the need to build a socialist state in Ghana, both to alleviate the country's own problems and social inequities and to serve as an example to other African states. He dedicates the book to "George Padmore (1900 [sic]-1959) and to the African Nation that must be," hoping to continue working to fulfill the dream of Padmore, W. E. B. DuBois, and other visionaries for a Union of African States.

Wright respected Padmore as an honest man whose dream of Pan-Africanism was exciting. Nevertheless, Wright's trip to Africa was to convince him that this dream, like other dreams, was perhaps impossible to realize. Africa, he felt, lacked men of George Padmore's stature.

When Wright left for Africa in 1953, he was still close to the *Présence Africaine* circle of black Africans in Paris that also kept close contact with Padmore. After his trip and after addressing[24] the First Congress of Negro Writers and Artists, sponsored by *Présence Africaine*, in Paris, September 1956, he began to move away from the ties he had with *Présence Africaine* writers. Wright did not attend the Second Congress held in Rome, March 1959, and by that time he had largely lost contact with the African writers in Paris. Nevertheless, his friendship with Padmore remained firm.

When George Padmore's best-known book was published in London, *Pan-Africanism or Communism?: The Coming Struggle for Africa* (1956), Wright contributed a foreword that showed his great admiration for the author.

Concerning George Padmore I am biased, for he is my friend. Yet, despite a personal relationship, I think that I can be objective about him. My admiration for him is evoked not only by his undeniable qualities, but by the objective position which he occupies in the minds of black people throughout the world.

George is, in my opinion, the greatest living authority on the fervent nationalist movements sweeping Black Africa today. Not only does he know those movements intimately, not only does he understand them in terms of their leaders, aims, structures, and ideologies, but George and his life *are those movements, aims and ideologies*.[25]

Padmore's influence continued; Wright expanded his interest in uniting the peoples of the world who shared the heavy yoke of political and economic oppression. In 1955 Wright traveled from Paris to Indonesia for the now historic Bandung Conference, a meeting of the independent nations of Asia and Africa to discuss racism and colonialism. Among the twenty-nine countries represented were China, India, Indonesia, Japan, Burma, Egypt, Turkey, the Philippines, Ethiopia, and the Gold Coast. Almost all the nations represented had been under Western domination in some form or other. This common bond of oppression would be taken up again years later by militants, Marxist in their sympathies, who called for a third-world coalition of Asian, African, and other nonwhite people against the racist and exploitative policies of the white Europeans and Americans.

Wright's impressions on the Bandung Conference were first published in a French translation (1955) and the following year in American and British editions as *The Color Curtain: A Report on the Bandung Conference*. In his foreword, Swedish sociologist Gunnar Myrdal, who helped Wright go to Indonesia, pointed out that this was a personal account of "a visiting stranger and a good reporter" on what he "saw there, and what he himself thought and felt." This kind of introduction seemed calculated to ward off the kind of criticism that *Black Power* had received for not being an authoritative study.

In 1957, *White Man, Listen!* was published in New York. This forebodingly-titled book contained four essays that warn of the catastrophe that can befall the Western world if it continues to deny human rights to large blocs of peoples. The essays, "The Psychological Reactions of Oppressed People," "Tradition and Industrialization," "The Literature of the Negro in the United States," and "The Miracle of Nationalism in the African Gold Coast," were delivered by Wright as lectures in many Western European cities during the years

1950-1956. These wide-ranging lectures recapitulate much of what their author had been saying or illustrating in earlier essays and books.

"The Psychological Reactions of Oppressed People" speaks of the missionary zeal which instilled in arrogant Europeans the belief that they could behave paternalistically toward more "primitive" cultures, and that they were justified in overrunning Asia, Africa, and much of America. Wright mentions Cortés's conquest of Montezuma as a drama of such European-induced confrontations of cultures. He sees "the white shadow of the West" falling across the rest of the world.

"Tradition and Industrialization" reviews the history of how Europeans plundered the economic resources of Asia and Africa. In this essay Wright points out that though he is a Westerner, conditioned to think as a Westerner, his race allows him a "double vision," and he is thus able to see the non-Western point of view.

"The Literature of the Negro in the United States" is an historical survey of black American authors. It includes considerations of Phyllis Wheatley, Paul Laurence Dunbar, W. E. B. DuBois, James Weldon Johnson, Claude McKay, Countee Cullen, and Langston Hughes. The essay refers directly and indirectly to what Wright had written many years before in *12 Million Black Voices*. Here again he takes issue with the word "Negro," paraphrasing a passage from the earlier book, and he quotes from the final pages of *12 Million Black Voices,* asserting black people's claim to a just share in the development of American life.

The last essay in the collection, "The Miracle of Nationalism in the African Gold Coast," traces the development of that area from a British colony to an independent nation: Ghana. Many of the problems of independence had previously been analyzed in *Black Power.*

White Man, Listen! was dedicated both to Eric Williams—a black friend who had become Chief Minister of the Government of Trinidad and Tobago—and to

> *the Westernized and tragic elite*
> *of Asia, Africa, and the West Indies—*
>
> the lonely outsiders who exist precariously
> on the clifflike margins of many cultures—men who
>   are
> distrusted, misunderstood, maligned, criticized
> by Left and Right, Christian and pagan—
> men who carry on their frail but indefatigable
>   shoulders
> the best of two worlds—and who,
> amidst confusion and stagnation,
> seek desperately for a home for their hearts:
> a home which, if found,
> could be a home for the hearts of all men.

Wright's most curious, most strange, and best book based upon his travels was *Pagan Spain* (New York, 1957), the result of short incursions into Spain in 1954 and 1955. He had considered returning to Africa, to visit other African countries, or taking a trip to Israel and Yugoslavia, but Gertrude Stein had suggested a visit to Spain, a "primitive, but lovely" land.[26] Then Alva and Gunnar Myrdal urged him to go to Spain, telling him he would be fascinated by that country's isolation from the rest of Europe, by its archaic institutions and modes of conservative thought, by its fanatic Catholicism, and by its broad acceptance of prostitution.

Few critics reviewed *Pagan Spain,* and those who did handed in negative reports. Nevertheless, the book was a strong and impressive account of the death of a country and its dreams of freedom. The atmosphere,

Wright found, was one that had long threatened to spread its pall over Mississippi and the whole of the United States.

Wright vividly recalled his *Daily Worker* articles about the Spanish Civil War and the Spanish Republic's efforts to survive the onslaught of General Francisco Franco's army and Adolf Hitler's bomber squadrons. Franco's victory ended the Civil War of 1936-1939. The Republic, established in 1931 to replace a dictatorship, was dead—and with its death freedom died too.

The Republican cause had been championed by intellectuals all over the world. Ernest Hemingway wrote about the war, as did George Orwell, Stephen Spender, Arthur Koestler, André Malraux, John Dos Passos, and many others who witnessed Spain's tragedy firsthand. (Wright's articles had been prepared without his ever having left the United States.) Poorly trained and poorly equipped idealists from other countries volunteered to fight in the International Brigades. It was a great crusade, and few volunteers minded much that the Brigades were largely controlled by Communists. The Republic's partisans saw the issue simply as Democracy versus Fascism. Franco and his supporters called for the restoration of "law and order" and the substitution of "strong government" for political factionalism.[27]

Wright felt very strongly that Franco's dictatorship had reimposed in Spain a form of mental enslavement not unlike that which had petrified the land during the Catholic Inquisition of 1492 and resulted in the Moors and Jews being driven out or underground. With the accession of Franco to power no religion other than Catholicism was permitted to function freely, and no political opposition to the regime was tolerated. Republican workers and writers not already imprisoned—or executed like the country's greatest contemporary poet, Federico García Lorca (1899-1936)—were watched closely to determine their political sympathies. Dissent meant arrest and long imprisonment without a fair trial.

What remained as Spain after the Inquisition was an "irrational paganism," says Wright, savagery that was to linger on through the ages as a "muddy residue." This "paganism" was only briefly interrupted or lessened by the short-lived Republic. The result of repression, whether it is in Jim Crow Mississippi or Franco Spain is, for the survivors, a living death in which existence becomes a nightmare—hopeless, never-ending.

Wright entitled his first chapter "Life After Death." This trip was a dream, a horrible nightmare, a calling up of underground emotions: fear and fire lynching the mind and body. It was Mississippi all over again. In Africa, Wright had been on foreign soil and he had felt it. In Spain he had been "at home," in the Mississippi of his youth.

In a strong sense, *Pagan Spain* was really about the emotional landscape of Mississippi. It was to lead Wright to turn again directly to Mississippi in *The Long Dream* (1958). He was to see that, for him, the best way to write on universal themes, to go beyond the racial theme, was to work through his roots and the fears that had formed him.

What Wright found in Spain fifteen years after Franco's victory were Civil Guards on street corners and railroad station platforms with machine guns; a land swarming with priests who milked it dry and received preferential treatment from the government; Protestants and Jews who were nonpersons, not permitted to worship openly; prostitutes patronized and tolerated by devout Catholics who on the other hand placed a high value on the pre-marital virginity of women; youths forced to memorize a catechism that said the glory and destiny of Spain was to spread Catholicism; dissenters reduced to whispers and newspapers reduced to praise or silence in the fear of suppression.

During his first days in Spain Wright visits a large, richly decorated cathedral with many shrines. His guides, two boys, point out a life-sized statue of the crucified Christ, commenting that it was He who gave Spain its many victories in war. Then they show him what must have impressed him as one of the more pagan, nightmarish aspects of Spanish Catholicism, the mummified remains of an honored bishop. Wright describes the horror that his hosts are evidently unaware of. "I saw sunken eye sockets, yellow, protruding teeth, and a mass of sagging, gray flesh falling away from the cranial structure of the head. The main portions of the body were mercifully hidden by a silken robe, though the forearms and hands, like white, running dough, were visible, and on the shrunken fingers were diamond rings. The boys crossed themselves and we went out wordlessly."[28] The specter of the bishop's mummified body haunts Wright, and on several occasions he asks Spaniards how they can accommodate such things with twentieth-century Christianity.

Wright has the same feeling of being detached from reality, of being in some kind of dream or nightmare world, when he travels to the famous shrine of the Black Virgin of Montserrat, near Barcelona. On the way he sees jutting out of the mountainside a series of rocky erections, "nations of seriated granite phalluses, tumefied and turgid . . . eternal distensions, until at last they became a kind of universe haunted by phallic images—images that were . . . obscenely bare and devoid

of all vegetation, filling the vision with vistas of a non-
or superhuman order of reality."[29]

Death fills his mind again when he witnesses the
best-known of Spain's pagan rituals: a bullfight. After
describing what he has seen, he asks why the human
heart hungers for this blood ritual, this sacrificial killing.
He calls the spectacle a "man-made agony to assuage
the emotional needs of men."

In Seville, Wright is startled by members of church
brotherhoods dressed for one of the innumerable religious festivals. Their white robes and tall, pointed hoods
give him "a creepy feeling," reminding him of the Ku
Klux Klan. Their flickering candles, like the rocky pro-
jections near the shrine of Montserrat, create for him
eery images of grotesque, unreal sexuality. The huge
candles drip white drops "like semen spraying, jutting
from the penises of sexually aroused bulls," and the
drums reverberate with a pagan, hypnotic beat as a
large sculptured Virgin is carried into view. Wright
makes the connection between hooded penitents protecting the Virgin and the Ku Klux Klan protecting
"the purity of white womanhood."[30]

The structure of *Pagan Spain* is curiously like that
of Wright's short story of the 1930's, "Fire and Cloud."
That story had a long section that alternated rhythmi-
cally between a black gospel preacher's exhortations
and the congregation's frenzied and approving re-
sponses. Here, the words of a religious and fascistic
catechism alternate with the prescribed response that is
to be memorized, not a gospel-style free response, but
just as uncritical. And Wright's comment on Spain's religious barbarism—in fact everything he writes here—is
a rebellious gospel parishioner's critical response called
up by the sermon or catechism.

The political catechism, portions of which Wright quotes at frequent intervals, is *Formación Politica: Lecciones para las Flechas*. A Spanish girl gives Wright the book and tells him she had to memorize it—all 176 pages of small print—before she was permitted to travel or work abroad. The cathecism is part of the six months of social work required of young women.

WHAT IS SPAIN?

Spain is a historical unit with a specific role to play in the world.

WHAT DOES THIS MEAN?

That destiny has constituted all the people of Spain, varied as they may be, for all time into a unit in the natural order of things.

WHAT IS A UNIT?

The union in one body of a number of distinct parts.

WHAT DOES DESTINY MEAN?

The purpose assigned to everyone in life.

WHAT IS MEANT BY THE NATURAL ORDER OF THINGS?

Something which concerns not only the Spanish but all nations.

WHAT THEN IS MEANT BY SAYING THAT SPAIN HAS BEEN FORMED BY DESTINY INTO A UNIT IN THE NATURAL ORDER OF THINGS?

Because it is a whole constituted from the various peoples who are united by the common destiny they have to fulfill in the world.

IS SPAIN OUR MOTHERLAND?

Yes.

. . . .

WHAT IS THIS DESTINY?

To include all men in a common movement for salvation.

WHAT DOES THIS MEAN?

Ensure that all men place spiritual values before material.

WHAT ARE SPIRITUAL VALUES?

> Firstly, religious values derived from our Catholic religion.

. . . .

HOW WILL SPAIN ACHIEVE ITS DESTINY?

> By the influence it exercises over other nations and also by conquest.

WHAT DO YOU MEAN BY INFLUENCE?

> Making others do something because they see us doing it.

WHAT DO YOU MEAN BY CONQUEST?

> To take possession by force of arms.

SINCE WHEN HAVE WE KNOWN THAT SPAIN HAS A DESTINY TO FULFILL?

> Since the most remote ages of its history.

GIVE SOME EXAMPLES

> [Nine examples are listed.]

AND FURTHER?

> [Four more examples are listed.][31]

After the startling, tragicomic material about the destiny of Spain, there is a section on feminine heroism. Here, in keeping with the Spanish *machismo,* the emphasis is on patience and obedience in the female.

DO WOMEN ALSO HAVE OPPORTUNITIES FOR HEROISM?

> Yes, though for them heroism consists more in doing well what they have to do every day than in dying heroically.

WHY?

> Because women haven't so much occasion to risk their lives.

ONLY FOR THIS?

> No, also because their temperament tends more to constant abnegation than to heroic deeds.

BUT ARE THERE SOME WHO HAVE GIVEN THEIR LIVES FOR THEIR COUNTRY?

Yes, because women do not shun their daily tasks
even if they cost them their lives.
WHAT DOES "SHUN" MEAN?
Flee, abandon one's obligations.[32]

The imagery, the dialogue, and the weaving of the
story of one man's Spain are skillful, the same elements
that make *Black Boy* and much of Wright's fiction so
powerful.

Pagan Spain was dedicated to Alva and Gunnar
Myrdal, "who suggested this book and whose compas-
sionate hearts have long brooded upon the degradation
of human life in Spain."

5

End of a Long Dream (1958-1960)

Pagan Spain led Richard Wright back to thoughts of Mississippi. One example of the degradation of human life had recalled another: both were part of the same universal tragedy that transcended problems of race or nationality. The following year Wright published *The Long Dream* (New York, 1958), written at a recently acquired old farmhouse in Ailly, Normandy. (Wright referred to this country retreat from the turbulence of life in Paris as a plot of land where he could grow himself some potatoes.) This novel, which so skillfully synthesized the style and themes of his earlier fiction, was to be the last book published in his lifetime. He died two years later, at the age of 52.

Like "Big Boy Leaves Home," *The Long Dream* begins with a black youngster at play in a circle of friends. The threatening white world around him remains vague and abstract until it forces him to grow up, to abandon childhood prematurely. He must either flee or share the burden of racism that crippled his father's manhood. Big Boy had fled north; *The Long Dream's* protagonist flees to France. Both men leave with a vague notion of the freedom to be found elsewhere.

In "Fire and Cloud" a black community leader who had lived according to the white establishment's rules was faced with a test. As his son watches him critically and learns from him, he confronts the crucial question: Dare he oppose the white mayor and chief of police and support a black demonstration, or must he remain a loyal establishment servant, an Uncle Tom? *The Long Dream* similarly portrays, quite skillfully, not only the pressure on a black community leader from the white mayor and the police chief he has always obeyed, but also a son's reactions to his father's way of dealing with the whites.

Rex Tucker, nicknamed Fishbelly, is a child from

a Mississippi black bourgeois family. His background is far from that of a Bigger Thomas. Rex's father, Tyree, makes a good living, principally from the operation of a funeral parlor. His mother, scarcely mentioned in the novel, is a good mother who loves her boy.

The only problem with this seemingly comfortable situation is that financial security has been won at a high price—the selling of one's soul. Tyree does what the white men tell him to do; in addition, by paying-off Chief of Police Cantley he is able to continue a lucrative sideline—a combination dance hall and whorehouse. His embalming work makes him a symbol of life after the death of freedom, and we are reminded of "pagan" Spain. In his mortuary work, in his selling of black women, and in his advice to his son, Tyree is burying black dreams of freedom. Speaking to his son, he says, "I make money by getting *black* dreams ready for burial. . . . A black man's a dream, son, a dream that can't come true. Dream, Fish. But be careful what you dream. Dream only what can happen."[1]

Dreams play an important part in this novel, which begins with Rex as a five-year-old just tucked into bed by his mother and dreaming of a big, angry fish trying to swallow him. Shortly afterward, he accompanies his father fishing, and watches him clean a catch by scooping out the entrails and bladder. Seizing the bladder, Rex blows it up like a balloon, and it reminds him of a pregnant woman's belly. As a joke, his friends and his father begin to call him Fishbelly, and the name sticks.

The fish dream and the circumstances surrounding Rex's acquisition of his new nickname foreshadow the sexual awakening of the black boy, his desire to have sex with a white woman precisely because it is the biggest white-imposed taboo he can break. "[H]e knew deep in his heart that there would be no peace in his blood until he had defiantly violated the line that the white world had dared him to cross under the threat of death."[2]

Fishbelly's father tries hard to indoctrinate him with his own way of life. Tyree takes him to a black whore so that he can develop a taste for black flesh rather than be tempted by the big white taboo, or by "foolish" ideas of equality. Such ideas are dangerous. One of Fishbelly's older friends, Chris, had been castrated and killed for sleeping with a white woman.

Fishbelly resents Tyree's way of life and hates his father for making him feel shame. He wants to break away, and ultimately does, but at the same time he loves his father.

A fire destroys Tyree's dance hall and takes the lives of forty-two people, including Fishbelly's light-skinned Negro mistress. Brushing aside his grief, Fish becomes businesslike. He offers to embalm all the bodies. Cantley is amused, "You and your papa are go-getters, aren't you? . . . You deal in hot meat, cold meat, and houses."[3]

The dance-hall fire results in demands that Tyree—who has allowed fire hazards to go uncorrected—be charged with criminal negligence or manslaughter. Tyree seeks to blackmail Cantley into helping him escape prosecution. He has carefully hidden canceled checks of graft payments to Cantley over a five-year period.

Unable to force Tyree to hand over the checks, Cantley kills him. In order to pressure Fishbelly into surrendering the evidence, the police chief sends a white girl to his room and has him jailed on a trumped-up sex charge.

Fishbelly is aided by a reform-minded lawyer, McWilliams, who tries to fight corruption and expose

Cantley. The lawyer has almost obtained Fishbelly's release when the latter discovers that his black cellmate
is a stool pigeon planted by Cantley. His assault on the
informer results in a two-year prison term.

When Fishbelly completes his sentence he is again
approached by Cantley, who is eager to make a deal
under which the black whorehouse and the police pay-
offs will be resumed. Fishbelly knows he must leave this
environment behind him. He finally becomes convinced
that his father was right after all, and that it is not possible for a Negro to be a man in Mississippi.

After turning over the incriminating evidence
against Cantley to McWilliams, Fishbelly goes to Memphis for a flight to New York and a connecting flight to
Paris. He tells McWilliams, "You are the only honest
white man I ever met," and he wonders if there is sufficient justice left in Mississippi to permit Cantley's conviction for some of his crimes.

Fishbelly kills no one; he is not Bigger Thomas or
Cross Damon. He prefers to leave an environment that
would in time destroy his manhood, or force him to
kill. A gentle man with anger welling up inside him—
much like Richard Wright himself—he follows the advice of friends and escapes to the sanctuary of France.
A childhood friend who had served in France during
the war and decided to remain there writes to Fishbelly
that "France ain't no heaven, but folks don't kill you
for crazy things."[4]

On the Memphis-New York plane, Fishbelly is
strapped into his seat by an attractive blond hostess,
and he holds his breath as his eyes scan her golden hair
and white skin. On the plane from New York to Paris,
he sees an attractive white woman sitting ahead of him,
but for two hours avoids looking at her, finally forcing
himself to stare directly at her. What makes this woman

a goddess men will protect with castration and murder?

An Italian-American on the plane tells Fishbelly he is on a trip to his father's birthplace, and he relates the story of his father's emigration to America, the land of opportunity. Fishbelly thinks to himself, "That man's father had come to America and had found a dream; he [Rex, alias Fishbelly] had been born in America and had found it a nightmare."[5] Could he ever make white people understand how they destroyed black lives?

The structure of *The Long Dream* is much stronger than that of *The Outsider,* and in one respect, stronger than that of *Native Son.* It does not digress into polemics, except perhaps for a two-page passage in which Tyree attempts to convince McWilliams that black corruption is justified in a white world.

Island of Hallucination, a completed but still unpublished sequel to *The Long Dream,* portrays Fishbelly in Paris, living among French and African intellectuals and other expatriate black Americans. It parallels Wright's own life by showing Fishbelly becoming involved in the intrigues, suspicions, and hostilities of the American and African black communities in Paris. Both the character and the author find this in-fighting more dangerous and nerve-racking than the open confrontations of Mississippi. The dangers are nonracial and subtle.

Wright, like Fishbelly, became increasingly fearful, not of French police chiefs, or of the French Communist Party, which resented his nonalignment with their positions, but of American CIA and Russian NKVD agents who he felt sure were spying on him. There was some justification for his fears. The same year that *The Outsider* was published in America, G. David Schine, a staff member of Senator Joseph McCarthy, visited Wright's Paris apartment to question him about Communist connections he had had in the United States. In succeeding years he received mysterious phone calls from people who gave fictitious names or misrepresented their business connections. Wright began to suspect other blacks of being secret agents. Rumors of who was or was not a spy poisoned the air and resulted in the exchange of angry accusations between friends. Were *Island of Hallucination* to be published today, the barely disguised suspicions Wright incorporated into his novel would probably cause new waves of recrimination within the circle of blacks still living in Paris.

There were good reasons for American and Russian agents to watch Richard Wright. Paris has traditionally been a center from which radical ideas spread, and Wright continued to speak out freely. His lectures emphasized ideas independent of either capitalist or Communist control—ideas that neither partner in the cold war cared to see students carry back to homes in various parts of the world.

Four of the lectures that Wright had delivered all over Western Europe had been published as *White Man, Listen!,* but the blunt yet eloquent and far-ranging speech he delivered to a study group at the American Church of Paris on November 8, 1960, remained unpublished. Wright entitled it "The Position of the Negro Artist and Intellectual in American Society," and in it he attacked a situation which forces black American authors to write for white publishers and a white audience. He assailed the American press and the American government for their attempts to prevent black expatriates from speaking out about problems in the United States. Wright reviewed for his audience his life and beliefs—Communism, Pan-Africanism, and Black Nationalism, his interest in sociology, and his sometimes strained relationships with the two other best-

known black American authors of the 1950's, Ralph
Ellison and James Baldwin.

Both 1959 and 1960 were unmitigatedly bad years
for Wright. *The Long Dream* had received negative reviews in the United States, where it was attacked with
particular severity by black critics who claimed that
Wright had lost his way and been cut off from his roots.
Although the French translations of his books were finding a receptive audience, not one of his works had received an enthusiastic response in America since 1945—
since *Black Boy*. His funds were low, and in 1959 he
was suffering from an amoebic infection he had picked
up somewhere on his travels. While ill and bedridden,
he began to compose three-line poems, Japanese haiku,
compiling 4,000 of them. His brother, Alan—now a
stranger whom he rarely thought about—wired from
Chicago that their mother had died of a stroke, but
Wright did not return to the United States for her funeral. He was alone much of the time, except for two
old friends, Chester Himes and Ollie Harrington, and
although by 1960 he had seemingly recovered from his
amoebic infection, his health continued to bother him.

In these years he received as visitors Dr. Martin
Luther King, Jr., Dorothy Padmore, whose husband,
George, had just died in Ghana, Arna Bontemps, and
E. Franklin Frazier, noted black American writers of
Negro history and sociology.

Not long after Wright's no-holds-barred speech at
the American Church of Paris, he became ill again. He
was admitted to the Clinique Chirugicale Eugène Gibez,
a small Parisian hospital, on November 26, 1960. He
was in good spirits but very tired from fighting the
grippe; he was to undergo examinations and get some
much-needed bed rest. At 11 p.m. on November 28 he
was found dead by the night nurse. The cause of death

was listed as a heart attack, his first and last. On December 3, Wright's body was cremated and the urn of
ashes deposited in a small corner of the columbarium in
Paris' Père Lachaise cemetery. Joining his ashes in the
creche were the ashes of a copy of *Black Boy*.

Wright's death and cremation caused the long-
submerged fears—many of which were shared by Wright
himself—of the black community in Paris to surface.
Rumors quickly spread that Wright had been poisoned.
But no proof of foul play could be found, and some
doubters reluctantly accepted the officially stated cause
of death. Others, however, continued for years to whis-
per their doubts in a frightened, nervous hush. One
well-known black writer embroidered and extended this
rumor into a novel that was published in the 1960's.
Was all this speculation part of the fabric of an island of
hallucination? All that can be said with certainty is that
the city Wright had said contained more freedom in one
block than in the whole of the United States had by the
end of his life become as much a place of fear as
Mississippi.

In the surging, turbulent 1960's, Wright's name
would be cited by American Black Power militants and
moderates alike, in a revival of interest in his work.
Stokely Carmichael, co-author with Charles V. Hamilton of *Black Power: The Politics of Liberation in America* (New York, 1967), spoke at Lincoln University,
the Pennsylvania school that trained such black leaders
as Langston Hughes, Supreme Court Justice Thurgood
Marshall, and Kwame Nkrumah. He urged the students
to read Richard Wright and Frederick Douglass, and to
rename their school after a black man—perhaps calling
it Frederick Douglass University, after a "real emanci-
pator" of black people.

Like Carmichael, Eldridge Cleaver pays high tribute to Richard Wright in the collection of essays, *Soul on Ice* (New York, 1968). "Of all black American novelists, and indeed of all American novelists of any hue, Richard Wright reigns supreme for his profound political, economic, and social reference."[6]

There is also a great respect for Wright among other black militants. In his autobiography, *Die Nigger Die!* (New York, 1969), H. Rap Brown says that Richard Wright—together with W. E. B. DuBois, Frederick Douglass, and Marcus Garvey—was a major influence on his thought. The greatest militant of all in the 1960's, Malcolm X, never met Wright but paid tribute to his memory by visiting Julia, Wright's oldest daughter, in Ghana, 1964; later he visited Ellen and Rachel, Wright's widow and second daughter, in Paris, and reported the occasion in his *Autobiography* (New York, 1965).

Black writers who have been deeply influenced by their inspirational father include James Baldwin, Ralph Ellison, and John A. Williams. Many were to see Wright as a black man concerned with human rights, who told it the way it really was, uncompromisingly.

The ambiguity of Fishbelly's existence in the last of Richard Wright's novels to be published before his death illustrates the dilemma of all Wright's other major fictional characters—and of Wright himself. Wright is speaking for many Fishbellys, many Bigger Thomases, and many other men who must live underground, hidden from themselves and others, when he says in *The Long Dream,* "His imagination had always pitted him physically against a personal enemy, but this enemy was vague, was part white, part black, was everywhere and nowhere, was within as well as without, and had allies in the shape of tradition, habit, and attitude."[7]

Wright's harsh experiences with cruelty—dream-like in quality, unreal and ambiguous—had made his life seem nightmarish. The infusion of this perception of reality into his writing gave his work its strength and its goals. Both strength and weaknesses came from an intense desire to detail and underscore the hell—the shadow world—a black man had to endure. At times he gave in to the temptation to editorialize, to polemicize, to arrest his narrative with abstract psychological or sociological comment; at other times he was able to combine a poetic lyricism with the harsh, brilliantly evocative prose of cruelty that made black readers say he was honest and accurate. That same prose made some white readers say Wright exaggerated; it was prose from which no white reader could receive cathartic release.

Richard Wright's literary reputation is increasing as the years pass and critics—most of them still white—begin to understand that his often rough style and content are a form of eloquence as admirable as another writer's smoothness. Wright fought with words and hit hard.

As a teacher, Wright taught that Marxism, Black Nationalism, and the unification of the world's nonwhite peoples against the virulence of white supremacy was the way out of an ambiguous existence in a white world.

The gray world of Richard Wright, with its fears and hopes, is more than the world of one man or of one race, although it is most keenly felt by those who have been taught to consider their black skin as a stigma. In the final analysis it is akin to the world endured by much of mankind in general. People search for a meaningful life and are frustrated by impersonal, accusing, and unseen powers. All too many are trapped in an existential hell, unable to correct or overcome the tragic flow of passing events. Cynicism and despair wage war against the hopes of a better world and of a place in that world that is clear and acceptable. The eternal struggle—political, economic, social, and psychological—continues . . .

Notes

1. Mississippi and Chicago (1908-1937)

1. *Black Boy: A Record of Childhood and Youth* (New York, 1945), pp. 143-144.
2. "The Ethics of Living Jim Crow: An Autobiographical Sketch," *American Stuff*, a WPA Writers' Anthology (New York, 1937), pp. 39-52; reprinted in the 1940 edition of *Uncle Tom's Children* and used almost in its entirety as an integral part of *Black Boy*.
3. *Atlantic Monthly*, CLXXIV (August 1944), 61-70, and (September 1944), 48-56; reprinted in *The God That Failed*, ed. Richard Crossman (New York, 1949), pp. 115-162.
4. Crossman, p. 118.
5. Crossman.
6. *New Masses*, X (June 26, 1934), 16.
7. *New Masses*, XV (April 30, 1935), 6.
8. *Partisan Review*, II (July-August 1935), 18-19.
9. *New Masses*, XVII (October 8, 1935), 18-19.
10. *New Masses*, XXVIII (July 5, 1938), 18-20.
11. *The New Caravan*, ed. Alfred Kreymborg (New York, 1936), pp. 124-158; reprinted in *Uncle Tom's Children: Four Novellas* (New York, 1938).

12.   Dan McCall, *The Example of Richard Wright* (New York, 1969), p. 6.

2.   *New York (1937-1947)*

1.   The original twenty-page draft of "Blueprint for Negro Literature" was revised and published in *New Challenge,* II (Fall 1937), 53-65. The longer, original version was published for the first time in *Amistad 2,* eds. John A. Williams and Charles F. Harris (New York, 1971), pp. 3-20.
2.   *Story Magazine,* XII (March 1938), 9-41; reprinted in *Uncle Tom's Children: Four Novellas,* 1938.
3.   *New Masses,* XXVII (May 10, 1938), 97-99, 116-124; reprinted in *Uncle Tom's Children: Five Long Stories,* 1940 edition.
4.   *New Masses,* XXIV (August 24, 1937), 19-20.
5.   *Harper's Bazaar,* LXXIV (January 1940), 40-41.
6.   Samuel Sillen, "The Response to 'Native Son,'" *New Masses,* XXXV (April 23, 1940), 25.
7.   *Native Son* (New York, 1940), pp. 24-25.
8.   *Ibid.,* p. 37.
9.   *Ibid.,* p. 79.
10. *Ibid.,* p. 201.
11. "How 'Bigger' Was Born," *Saturday Review of Literature,* XXII (June 1, 1940), 19. The article was a shortened version of a lecture Wright gave at the Harlem branch of the New York Public Library. The full lecture was published by Harper (1940), and is currently available in *Black Voices: An Anthology of Afro-American Literature,* ed. Abraham Chapman (New York, 1968), pp. 538-563.
12. *Native Son,* p. 242.
13. *Ibid.,* p. 281.
14. *Ibid.,* p. 333.
15. *Ibid.,* p. 358.

16. *Ibid.*, p. 359. The ellipses in the passage quoted are Wright's.
17. *12 Million Black Voices: A Folk History of the Negro in the United States* (New York, 1941), p. 30.
18. *Ibid.*, p. 13.
19. *Ibid.*, p. 15.
20. *Ibid.*, pp. 68-73.
21. *Ibid.*, pp. 35, 144.
22. *Ibid.*, p. 27.
23. Michel Fabre, "Richard Wright: The Man Who Lived Underground," *Studies in the Novel,* III (Summer 1971), 166-167.
24. "Two Excerpts from a Novel," *Accent,* II (Spring 1942), 170-176.
25. "The Man Who Lived Underground," *Cross Section 1944,* ed. Edwin Seaver (New York, 1944), pp. 58-102. The novelette was included in Wright's collection *Eight Men* (New York, 1961), pp. 27-92. Page citations will be to *Eight Men.* The story is currently available in *Black Voices: An Anthology of Afro-American Literature* (mentioned above in footnote 11), pp. 114-160; and in a bilingual edition, *The Man Who Lived Underground/ L'Homme qui vivait sous terre,* ed. Michel Fabre, translated by Claude-Edmonde Magny (Paris, 1971).
26. Fabre, pp. 166-167.
27. "The Man Who Lived Underground," *Eight Men,* p. 34.
28. *Ibid.*, p. 70.
29. *Ibid.*, p. 78.
30. *The God That Failed,* pp. 145-146.
31. *Ibid.*, p. 162.
32. *Ibid.*
33. *Black Boy,* pp. 7, 63-64.
34. St. Clair Drake and Horace R. Cayton, *Black Metropolis: A Study of Negro Life in a Northern City,* 2 vols., rev. ed. (New York, 1962), pp. xx-xxi. The

study, with Wright's introduction, was first published in 1945.

35. Published together with two other essays by Wright, under the general title "Discrimination in America," *Twice a Year,* XIV-XV (Fall 1946-Winter 1947).

36. James Joyce, *A Portrait of the Artist as a Young Man* (New York, 1956, originally published 1916), pp. 246-247.

3. Paris (1947-1952)

1. Constance Webb, *Richard Wright: A Biography* (New York, 1968), notes, p. 419.

2. *Ibid.,* p. 294.

3. " 'Native Son' Filmed in Argentina," *Ebony,* VI (January 1951), 83.

4. "The Shame of Chicago," *Ebony,* VII (December 1951), 24-31.

5. Webb, pp. 292-304.

6. *"L'Homme qui tua une ombre," Les Lettres Françaises* (October 4, 1946), translated by André Villars; "The Man Who Killed a Shadow," *Zero,* I (Spring 1949), 45-53; reprinted in *Eight Men* (1961).

7. "Big Black Good Man" was first published in *Esquire,* L (November 1957), 76-80; reprinted in *Eight Men;* "Man, God Ain't Like That . . ." and "Man of All Work" were first published in *Eight Men.*

4. Paris (1953-1957)

1. *The Outsider* (New York, 1953), p. 92.

2. *Ibid.,* p. 17. The ellipsis in the passage quoted is Wright's.

3. *Ibid.,* pp. 17-18.

4. *Ibid.,* p. 342.

5. *Ibid.,* p. 21.

6. *Ibid.*, p. 125.
7. *Ibid.*, p. 347.
8. *Ibid.*, p. 173.
9. Wright's ellipsis.
10. *Ibid.*, p. 264.
11. *Ibid.*, p. 404.
12. *Ibid.*, p. 123.
13. *Ibid.*, p. 126.
14. *Ibid.*, pp. 324-338.
15. Wright's ellipsis.
16. Wright's ellipsis.
17. Wright's ellipsis.
18. *Ibid.*, p. 404.
19. *Ibid.*, p. 405. The ellipses are Wright's.
20. McCall, pp. 147-148.
21. *Black Power: A Record of Reactions in a Land of Pathos* (New York, 1954), p. 347. The ellipsis in the passage quoted is Wright's.
22. *Ibid.*, p. 348.
23. Léopold Sédar Senghor, "Négritude and Marxism," *Africa in Prose,* eds. O. R. Dathorne and Willfried Feuser (Baltimore, 1969), p. 343.
24. Richard Wright, "Tradition and Industrialization, the Plight of the Tragic Elite in Africa," *Présence Africaine,* No. 8-9-10 (June-November 1956), 347-360, later included in *White Man, Listen!* (1957). The same issue includes, among many other papers read to the First Congress of Negro Writers and Artists, *"Racisme et culture,"* by Frantz Fanon, the black Algerian psychoanalyst born in Martinique, pp. 122-131, and *"Culture et colonisation,"* by Aimé Césaire, poet-statesman from Martinique, pp. 190-205.
25. Richard Wright, "Foreword," in George Padmore, *Pan-Africanism or Communism?: The Coming Struggle for Africa* (London, 1956), p. 11.
26. *Pagan Spain* (New York, 1957), pp. 1-2.
27. The most comprehensive of innumerable books on the Spanish Civil War is Hugh Thomas, *The Spanish*

Civil War (New York, 1961). For a few studies of writers' involvement in the War, see Allen Guttmann, *The Wound in the Heart: America and the Spanish Civil War* (New York, 1962); Hugh Ford, *A Poet's War: British Poets and the Spanish Civil War* (Philadelphia, 1965); Stanley Weintraub, *The Last Great Cause: The Intellectuals and the Spanish Civil War* (New York, 1968). A fascinating personal memoir of the war is George Orwell, *Homage to Catalonia* (New York, 1952, originally published in London, 1938).

28. *Pagan Spain,* p. 10.
29. *Ibid.,* p. 61.
30. *Ibid.,* p. 237.
31. *Ibid.,* pp. 22-24.
32. *Ibid.,* p. 77.

5.   *End of a Long Dream (1958-1960)*

1. *The Long Dream* (Garden City, N.Y., 1958), p. 79.
2. *Ibid.,* p. 157.
3. *Ibid.,* p. 227.
4. *Ibid.,* p. 372.
5. *Ibid.,* p. 380.
6. Eldridge Cleaver, "Notes on a Native Son," *Soul on Ice* (New York, 1968), p. 108.
7. *The Long Dream,* pp. 252-253.

Bibliography

Original Editions of Wright's Books

Uncle Tom's Children. New York: Harper, 1938.
Native Son. New York: Harper, 1940.
12 Million Black Voices: A Folk History of the Negro in the United States. New York: Viking, 1941.
Black Boy: A Record of Childhood and Youth. New York: Harper, 1945.
The Outsider. New York: Harper, 1953.
Savage Holiday. New York: Avon, 1954.
Black Power: A Record of Reactions in a Land of Pathos. New York: Harper, 1954.
The Color Curtain: A Report on the Bandung Conference. Cleveland and New York: World, 1956.
Pagan Spain. New York: Harper, 1957.
White Man, Listen! Garden City, N.Y.: Doubleday, 1957.
The Long Dream. Garden City, N.Y.: Doubleday, 1958.
Eight Men. Cleveland and New York: World, 1961.
Lawd Today. New York: Walker, 1963.

Principal Essays

"The Ethics of Living Jim Crow: An Autobiographical
Sketch," *American Stuff,* a WPA Writers' Anthology.
New York: Viking, 1937. Pp. 39-52.

"Blueprint for Negro Writing," *New Challenge,* II (Fall
1937), 53-65. The longer, original version was published for the first time in *Amistad 2,* eds. John A.
Williams and Charles F. Harris. New York: Vintage,
1971. Pp. 3-20.

"How 'Bigger' Was Born," *Saturday Review of Literature,*
XXII (June 1, 1940), 3-4ff. The longer, original version was published in booklet form, New York: Harper, 1940.

"I Tried To Be a Communist," *Atlantic Monthly,* CLXXIV
(August 1944), 61-70, and (September 1944), 48-56.

"Early Days in Chicago," *Cross-Section,* ed. Edwin Seaver.
New York: L. B. Fischer, 1945. Pp. 306-342.

"Introduction" to *Black Metropolis: A Study of Negro Life
in a Northern City,* by St. Clair Drake and Horace R.
Cayton. New York: Harcourt, Brace, 1945. Pp. xvii-
xxxiv.

"The Position of the Negro Artist and Intellectual in
American Society," 1960, unpublished.

Bibliographies of Wright's Publications

Sprague, M. D. "Richard Wright: A Bibliography," *Bulletin of Bibliography,* XXI (September-December
1953), 39.

Fabre, Michel, and Margolies, Edward. "Richard Wright
(1908-1960): A Bibliography," *Bulletin of Bibliography,* XXIV (January-April 1965), 131-133, 137.
Reprinted as an appendix to Constance Webb's biography of Wright, mentioned below. Reprinted a second time in the January 1969 issue of *Negro Digest.*

Fabre, Michel, and Margolies, Edward. "A Bibliography
of Richard Wright's Works," *New Letters,* XXXVIII

(Winter 1971), 155-169. A revised and enlarged version of the bibliography first published in *Bulletin of Bibliography*, 1965.

Biographies

Webb, Constance. *Richard Wright: A Biography*. New York: G. P. Putnam's Sons, 1968.

Williams, John A. *The Most Native of Sons*. Garden City, N.Y.: Doubleday, 1970.

Critical Works of Special Interest

Margolies, Edward. *The Art of Richard Wright*. Carbondale: Southern Illinois University Press, 1969.

McCall, Dan. *The Example of Richard Wright*. New York: Harcourt, Brace & World, 1969.

Bone, Robert. *Richard Wright*. Minneapolis: University of Minnesota, 1969 (pamphlet).

Brignano, Russell Carl. *Richard Wright: An Introduction to the Man and His Works*. Pittsburgh: University of Pittsburgh Press, 1970.

Bibliographies of Criticism on Wright

Bryer, Jackson. "Richard Wright (1908-1960): A Selected Check List of Criticism," *Wisconsin Studies in Contemporary Literature,* I (Fall 1960), 22-33.

Abcarian, Richard, ed. *Richard Wright's "Native Son": A Critical Handbook*. Belmont, Cal.: Wadsworth Publishing Company, 1970 (contains bibliographical appendix).

Brignano, Russell C. "Richard Wright: A Bibliography of Secondary Sources," *Studies in Black Literature,* II (Summer 1971), 19-24.

Reilly, John M. "Richard Wright: An Essay in Bibliography," *Resources for American Literary Study,* I (Autumn 1971), 131-180.

Index

Africa Must Unite (Nkrumah), 77
African Culture, 41–42, 56, 61, 75–81
"Almos' a Man," 29–30
American Dilemma, An (Myrdal), 53
America's Coming-of-Age (Brooks), 14
Aswell, Edward, 57, 74
Autobiography (Malcolm X), 98

Baldwin, James, 52, 56, 96, 98
Beauvoir, Simone de, 57
"Between the World and Me," 10–11
"Big Black Good Man," 61, 62, 104 n. 7
"Big Boy Leaves Home," 8, 12, 19
    The Long Dream and, 90
    Native Boy and, 22
Black Boy: A Record of

Childhood and Youth, xiii, 3, 5–6, 7, 40, 49–52, 64, 88, 96–97
Black Metropolis, Introduction to, xiii, 51–52
Black Power: The Politics of Liberation in America (Carmichael-Hamilton), 97
Black Power: A Record of Reactions in a Land of Pathos, xiii, 4–5, 40, 42, 75–76, 79, 81
Blake, William, 67
"Blueprint for Negro Literature," 18
Bontemps, Arna, 96
"Bright and Morning Star," 19, 22, 25–28, 42
Brooks, Van Wyck, 14
Browder, Earl, 28
Brown, H. Rap, 98

Camus, Albert, 45, 58, 65
Canfield, Cass, 30

Carmichael, Stokely, 97
Césaire, Aimé, 57
Chenal, Pierre, 59
Cleaver, Eldridge, 97–98
Color Curtain: A Report on the Bandung Conference, The, xiii, 4–5, 79
Communism, xi–xii, 3–4, 7–11, 16, 18–19, 31, 48–49, 53, 79, 82, 94–95, 99
  religion and, 42, 53
  Wright's writings and, 22, 24–28, 33, 42–43, 68–69, 76
Conrad, Joseph, 45
Crime and Punishment (Dostoyevsky), 69
Crosby, George, 59
Cullen, Countee, 80

Damas, Léon, 57
Davis, Benjamin, Jr., xii, 18
Die Nigger Die! (Brown), 98
Diop, Alioune, 57
"Discrimination in America," 104 n. 35
Dixon, Dean, 56
Dos Passos, John, 82
Dostoyevsky, Feodor, 45, 69
Douglass, Frederick, 97–98
"Down by the Riverside," 19, 28–29
Dreiser, Theodore, x, 7
DuBois, W. E. B., 77, 80, 98
Dunbar, Paul Laurence, 80

Eight Men, xiv, 29, 64
Eliot, T. S., 14

Ellison, Ralph, xii, 30, 43, 96, 98
"Ethics of Living Jim Crow, The," 6, 19
Étranger, L' (Camus), 65

Ferenczi, Sandor, 73
"Fire and Cloud," 18, 19, 22, 42, 85
  The Long Dream and, 90
Fire Next Time, The (Baldwin), 52
Ford, James, 18
Franco, Francisco, 82
Frank, Waldo, 14
Frazier, E. Franklin, 96
Freud, Sigmund, 67, 73

García Lorca, Federico, 83
Garvey, Marcus, 98
Gentry, Herb, 56
Gide, André, 58
Green, Paul, 58

Hamilton, Charles V., 97
Harrington, Ollie, 56, 96
Haynes, Leroy, 56
Heart of Darkness (Conrad), 45, 47
Heath, Gordon, 56
Hemingway, Ernest, 82
Himes, Chester, 56, 96
Hitler, Adolf, 52
"How 'Bigger' Was Born," 35, 38, 102 n. 11
Hughes, Langston, 80, 97
Humor, 61–62

"I Have Seen Black Hands," 9–10

"I Tried to Be a Commu-
        nist," xii, 8, 49
Invisible Man (Ellison), 43,
        47–48
Island of Hallucination, xiv,
        94–95

Japanese haiku, 96
"Joe Louis Uncovers Dyna-
        mite," 11
Johnson, Jack, 15
Johnson, James Weldon, 80
Joyce, James, 13–14, 53

King, Martin Luther, Jr., 96
Koestler, Arthur, 82

Last Flight, The (film), 59
Lawd Today, 13–15, 66
Lee, Canada, 58
Lenin, N., 9
"Letter to International
        Publishers, A," 28
Lewis, Joe, 11
Lewis, Sinclair, x, 7
"Long Black Song," 19–20
    Native Son and, 22
Long Dream, The, xiii, 64,
        83, 90–94, 96, 98
    "Big Boy Leaves Home"
        and, 90
    "Fire and Cloud" and, 90
    Native Son and, 94
    The Outsider and, 94
Lorca, *see* García Lorca

McCarthy, Joseph, 94
McKay, Claude, 80
Malcolm X, 98
Malraux, André, 82
"Man, God Ain't Like
        That. . . ," 61–62

"Man of All Work," 61, 62
"Man Who Killed a
        Shadow, The," 60
*Man Who Lived Under-
        ground, The,* xii, 40,
        43, 44–48, 61, 65–
        66, 69, 72
    The Outsider and, 72
"Man Who Saw the Flood,
        The," *see* "Silt"
"Man Who Was Almost a
        Man, The," *see* "Al-
        mos' a Man"
Marshall, Thurgood, 97
Marx, Karl, 9
Meadman (Wright), Rose
        Dhima, xii, 30, 53,
        74
Melody Unlimited (film),
        59
Mencken, H. L., x, 7
Myrdal, Gunnar, 53, 79, 81,
        88

NAACP, xii, 32
Native Son (film), xiii, 58–
        59, 64
Native Son (novel), xii, 3,
        5, 11, 22, 30–35, 44,
        48, 51–52, 60–61,
        64, 65–66, 69
    The Long Dream and, 94
    The Outsider and, 65,
        69–71
Native Son (stage), xii, 58–
        59
"Negroes in Manhattan," xi,
        18
Nkrumah, Kwame, 76, 77,
        97
Nurse, Malcolm, *see* George
        Padmore

Orwell, George, 82
Our America (Frank), 14
Outsider, The, xiii, 5, 38,
    64–65, 75
  The Long Dream and, 94
  Native Son and, 65

Padmore, Dorothy, 96
Padmore, George, 76–78,
    96
Pagan Spain, xiii, 5, 81–88,
    90
*Pan-Africanism or Commu-
    nism?* (Padmore), 78
Poplar (Wright), Ellen, xii,
    53, 98
"Portrait of the Artist as a
    Young Man, A"
    (Joyce), 53
"Position of the Negro Art-
    ist and Intellectual in
    American Society,
    The," 95
Potter, Larry, 56

"Red Leaves of Red Books,"
    10
Reik, Theodore, 74
Religion, 83–84
  in *Black Power,* 42
  in "Bright and Morning
    Star," 25–27, 42
  in "Fire and Cloud," 42,
    85
  in "Long Black Song," 21
  in "Man, God Ain't Like
    That. . . ," 61
  in *The Man Who Lived
    Underground,* 44–45
  in *Native Son,* 22–25,
    35–37

in *The Outsider,* 66–68
in *Pagan Spain,* 85
Reynolds, Paul R., 72, 74
Roosevelt, Franklin Delano,
    28
Rosskam, Edwin, 40

Sartre, Jean-Paul, 45, 57–58
Savage Holiday, xiii, 72–75
Schine, G. David, 94
Senghor, Léopold Sédar, 58,
    76
Sex, 85
  in "Long Black Song," 20
  in "Man of All Work," 62
  in "The Man Who Killed
    a Shadow," 60
  in *Native Son,* 33–34
  in *Savage Holiday,* 73
"Shame of Chicago, The,"
    59
"Silt," 29
Simmons, Art, 56
Smith, William Gardner, 56
Spender, Stephen, 82
Stein, Gertrude, 57, 81
Sunday Neuroses (Ferenczi),
    73
"Superstition," xi, 8

Totem and Taboo (Freud),
    67, 73–74
12 Million Black Voices, xii,
    40, 42–43, 72
  Black Power and, 76, 80

Ulysses (Joyce), 13–14
Uncle Tom's Children, xi–
    xii, 3, 5, 13, 19, 22–
    30, 35
Unknown Murderer, The
    (Reik), 74

"Urban Misery in an American City," 52–53

Violence, 22, 51–52
in "Almos' a Man," 30
in "Bright and Morning Star," 27
in "The Man Who Killed a Shadow," 60
in *Native Son,* 3, 24, 31–37
in *The Outsider,* 65–68
in *Savage Holiday,* 73
"Voodoo of Hell's Half-Acre, The," x, 8

Waste Land, The (Eliot), 14
Wheatley, Phyllis, 80

White Man, Listen!, xiii, 4–5, 38, 71, 79–81, 95
Williams, John A., 98
Wright, Ellen Poplar, xii, 53, 98
Wright, Julia, xii, 53, 57, 98
Wright, Rachel, xiii, 64, 98
Wright, Richard
awards, xi–xii, 30, 31
birth, ix
death, xiv, 90, 96–97
early life, ix–xi, 3–6
marriages, xii, 30, 53
in New York, 18–54
in Paris, xiii, 53, 56–97
Wright, Rose Dhima Meadman, xii, 30, 53, 74